Pubs & Inns

2009

of Britain

- Including Family-friendly & Dog-friendly Pubs
- Accommodation, food and traditional good-cheer

Foxhunters Inn, Ilfracombe, Devon

Foreword

Since early times there have been inns and taverns to cater for the traveller, and for the working man (and woman) needing refreshment after a hard and gruelling day. Some of these inns and taverns still exist today, along with numerous, more recently built pubs and small hotels, all of which offer the traveller, and the casual or regular visitor, the chance to rest, enjoy good food and drink, and exchange pleasantries with friends and new acquaintances.

In **Pubs & Inns of Britain** 2009 you will find a number of such establishments where you can stop for meal or a drink, or even for a longer stay. Refer to our Pet Friendly or Family Friendly Supplements on pages 174 to 186 if you are travelling with children or pets, or use our Readers' Offer Vouchers on pages 187-218 to save money on family outings.

Anne Cuthbertson
Editor

© FHG Guides Ltd, 2009
ISBN 978-1-85055-410-3

Maps: ©MAPS IN MINUTES™ / Collins Bartholomew 2007

Typeset by FHG Guides Ltd, Paisley.
Printed and bound in China by Imago.

Distribution. Book Trade: ORCA Book Services, Stanley House,
3 Fleets Lane, Poole, Dorset BH15 3AJ
(Tel: 01202 665432; Fax: 01202 666219)
e-mail: mail@orcabookservices.co.uk
Published by FHG Guides Ltd., Abbey Mill Business Centre,
Seedhill, Paisley PA1 ITJ (Tel: 0141-887 0428 Fax: 0141-889 7204).
e-mail: admin@fhguides.co.uk

Recommended Inns & Pubs of Britain is published by FHG Guides Ltd,
part of Kuperard Group.

Cover design: FHG Guides
Cover Picture: courtesy of Britannia Inn, Langdale (full details page 129)

Contents

SOUTH WEST ENGLAND
5

Cornwall, Devon, Dorset
Gloucestershire, Somerset, Wiltshire

LONDON & SOUTH EAST ENGLAND
36

London (Central & Greater),
Berkshire, Buckinghamshire,
Hampshire, Isle of Wight, Kent,
Oxfordshire, Surrey,
East Sussex, West Sussex

EAST OF ENGLAND
61

Bedfordshire, Cambridgeshire,
Essex, Hertfordshire, Norfolk, Suffolk

MIDLANDS
79

Derbyshire, Herefordshire,
Leicestershire & Rutland, Lincolnshire
Northamptonshire, Nottinghamshire,
Shropshire, Staffordshire,
Warwickshire, Worcestershire

YORKSHIRE
97

East Yorkshire, North Yorkshire,
South Yorkshire

NORTH EAST ENGLAND
107

Northumberland, Tyne & Wear

NORTH WEST ENGLAND
115

Cheshire, Cumbria, Lancashire,
Greater Manchester

SCOTLAND

WALES

England and Wales · Counties

1. Plymouth	12. Windsor & Maidenhead	23. Milton Keynes	34. Blackpool	
2. Torbay	13. Bracknell Forest	24. Peterborough	35. N.E. Lincolnshire	
3. Poole	14. Wokingham	25. Leicester	36. North Lincolnshire	
4. Bournemouth	15. Reading	26. Nottingham	37. Kingston-upon-Hull	
5. Southampton	16. West Berkshire	27. Derby	38. York	
6. Portsmouth	17. Swindon	28. Telford & Wrekin	39. Redcar & Cleveland	
7. Brighton & Hove	18. Bath & Northeast Somerset	29. Stoke-on-Trent	40. Middlesborough	
8. Medway	19. North Somerset	30. Warrington	41. Stockton-on-Tees	
9. Thurrock	20. Bristol	31. Halton	42. Darlington	
10. Southend	21. South Gloucestershire	32. Merseyside	43. Hartlepool	
11. Slough	22. Luton	33. Blackburn with Darwen		

NORTH WALES
a. Denbighshire
b. Flintshire
c. Wrexham

SOUTH WALES
d. Swansea
e. Neath & Port Talbot
f. Bridgend
g. Rhondda Cynon Taff
h. Merthyr Tydfil
i. Vale of Glamorgan
j. Cardiff
k. Caerphilly
l. Blaenau Gwent
m. Torfaen
n. Newport
o. Monmouthshire

Cornwall

Set in a working fishing cove at the bottom of a steep village, this 300-year old inn is a favourite with ramblers and holidaymakers alike.

There are 6 letting bedrooms, some en suite, and most with stunning sea views.

Locally sourced seafood, including lobster in season, crab and bass, features strongly on the well-balanced menus, which cater for all tastes, including vegetarian.

CADGWITH COVE INN

enquiries@cadgwithcoveinn.com
www.cadgwithcoveinn.com

There is a good selection of cask ales, including Cornish brews, and a regularly changing wine list.

Well-behaved dogs are welcome.

The Inn is situated off the A3083 between Helston and The Lizard

CADGWITH COVE INN

**Cadgwith Cove, Helston,
Cornwall TR12 7JX
Tel: 01326 290513
Fax: 01326 291018**

6 BEDROOMS, 3 WITH PRIVATE BATHROOM. PUNCH HOUSE WITH REAL ALE. CHILDREN AND PETS WELCOME. BAR AND RESTAURANT MEALS. NON-SMOKING AREAS. LIZARD 3 MILES. S££, D££.

THE RISING SUN INN

Altarnun, Launceston, Cornwall PL15 7SN • Tel: 01566 86332

The Rising Sun is a country pub and has retained many features from its origins as a 16th century inn. It is the ideal place to escape to for a pint of your favourite ale, a game of dart or pool - and don't miss the home-cooked burgers, lasagne, fish dishes and meat pies.

Reportedly the oldest Inn in Cornwall, nestling in the pretty village of Perranuthnoe, with its sandy beach and access to the scenic South West Coastal Path. A traditional country pub with oak floors, wood burner, beams and granite walls, the varied menu focuses on fresh local seafood and Cornish-reared meat, with all tastes catered for. Meals available lunchtimes and evenings together with an extensive wine list and range of real ales. Letting accommodation comprises two double rooms, both with en suite shower.

THE VICTORIA INN
Perranuthnoe, Near Penzance, Cornwall TR20 9NP
Tel: 01736 710309 • Fax: 01736 719284
e-mail: enquiries@victoriainn-penzance.co.uk • www.victoriainn-penzance.co.uk

2 BEDROOMS, BOTH WITH EN SUITE SHOWER. ALL BEDROOMS NON-SMOKING. PUBFOLIO HOUSE WITH REAL ALE. CHILDREN AND PETS WELCOME. BAR AND RESTAURANT MEALS. PENZANCE 4 MILES. S££, D£.

RATES

S – SINGLE ROOM rate   D – Sharing DOUBLE/TWIN ROOM

S£ D£ =Under £35   S££ D££ =£36-£45   S£££ D£££ =£46-£55   S££££ D££££ =Over £55

This is meant as an indication only and does not show prices for Special Breaks, Weekends, etc.
Guests are therefore advised to verify all prices on enquiring or booking.

THE *New Inn*

Veryan, Truro, Cornwall TR2 5QA

Set in a picturesque village on the Roseland Peninsula, the New Inn is a small granite pub, originally consisting of two cottages and was built in the 16th century.

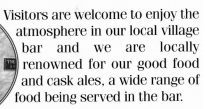

Visitors are welcome to enjoy the atmosphere in our local village bar and we are locally renowned for our good food and cask ales, a wide range of food being served in the bar.

Accommodation consists of spacious and comfortable rooms – one single with separate private facilities, and one double and one twin en suite. St Austell and Truro are nearby, and we are situated close to the beautiful sandy beaches of Pendower and Carne.

Tel: 01872 501362 • Fax: 01872 501078 • www.newinnveryan.co.uk

3 BEDROOMS, ALL WITH PRIVATE BATHROOM. FREE HOUSE WITH REAL ALE. BAR MEALS. MEVAGISSEY 7 MILES. S££, D££.

Cornwall receives most of its visitors over the summer months, exploring the beautiful beaches and indulging in the exceptional clotted cream teas - but the county has much to offer besides the Cornish pastie and the traditional bucket and spade holiday. The "shoulder" and winter months offer opportunities for the discerning visitor which may go unnoticed in the annual stampede to the beaches. There are villages boasting curious and ancient names - Come To Good, Ting Tang, London Apprentice and Indian Queens, often sporting parish churches, ancient graveyards and distinctive crosses which reveal their early Christian history. Wayside crosses, holy wells and Celtic stone circles are reminders that the Cornish are true Celts - it was they who embossed the headlands with cliff forts to repel marauders.

To discover more about life in the Iron Age there are numerous settlements to visit, for example Castle an Dinas, one of the largest preserved hill forts in Cornwall. Alternatively Chysauster Ancient Village is a deserted Roman village comprising eight well-preserved houses around an open court. More up-to-date is St Michael's Mount with its 14th century castle, or Prideaux Place, a stunning Elizabethan House, and Lanhydrock, the National Trust's most visited property in Cornwall, which was once the residence of a local family whose wealth came from tin mining.

Devon

Dartmoor Lodge
Peartree Cross, Ashburton, Devon, TQ13 7JW
Tel: 01364 652 232 • 01364 653 990 • www.dartmoorlodge.com
There is no better place for walkers and lovers of wide-open spaces, with the attractions of the National Park on the doorstep. It is positioned equidistant between Plymouth and Exeter, both superb for culture and shopping. Dartmoor Lodge caters for every occasion, with modern facilities in both function suites as well as in the bedrooms.

The Cedars Inn
Bickington Road, Barnstaple, Devon EX31 2HE
Tel: 01271 371 784 • Fax: 01271 325 733 • www.cedarsinn-barnstaple.com
Just a short distance from the Devon coastline and ideal for cyclists taking the Tarka Trail, the inn is an ideal base for exploring or for observing the local wildlife. Accommodation is in lodge form, with single, double, twin and family rooms available. Each room is en suite, with a range of facilities including colour TV, stereo system and telephone.

THE DARTBRIDGE INN
Totnes Road, Buckfastleigh, Devon TQ11 0JR
Tel: 01364 642 214 •01364 643 839 • www.dartbridgeinn.com
With a number of day-trip attractions nearby, this comfortable inn provides ground floor accommodation in a variety of double and twin rooms, with Z-beds and cots available on request. Fine wines and coffees, lunchtime snacks, and dishes featuring locally caught fish are obtainable all day everyday in the bar and restaurant.

The Weary Ploughman
Dartmouth Road, Churston Ferrers, Brixham, Devon TQ5 0LL
Tel: 01803 844 702 • www.wearyploughman.co.uk
Originally a railway hotel, this pub/ restaurant/ hotel provides locals and business persons with a relaxing sanctuary in which to eat, drink, and relax. There is a good selection of fine wines and ales in the bar, freshly prepared fare in the restaurant and de luxe accommodation at an affordable price.

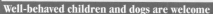
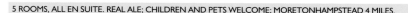

Devon is unique, with two different coastlines: bare rugged cliffs, white pebble beaches, stretches of golden sands, and the Jurassic Coast, England's first natural World Heritage Site. Glorious countryside: green rolling hills, bustling market towns and villages, thatched, white-washed cottages and traditional Devon longhouses. Wild and wonderful moorland: Dartmoor, in the south, embraces wild landscapes and picture-postcard villages; Exmoor in the north combines breathtaking, rugged coastline with wild heather moorland. Step back in time and discover historic cities, myths and legends, seafaring characters like Drake and Raleigh, and settings for novels by Agatha Christie and Conan Doyle.

Devon is home to an amazing and diverse range of birds. Enjoy special organised birdwatching trips, perhaps on board a RSPB Avocet Cruise or a vintage tram. Devon is the walking county of the South West – imagine drifts of bluebells lit by dappled sunlight, the smell of new mown hay, the sound of the sea, crisp country walks followed by a roaring fire and hot 'toddies'! If pedal power is your choice, you will discover exciting off-road cycling, leisurely afternoon rides, and challenging long distance routes such as the Granite Way along Dartmoor, the Grand Western Canal and the coastal Exmouth to Budleigh Circuit.

12 BEDROOMS, ALL WITH PRIVATE BATHROOM. REAL ALE. BAR AND RESTAURANT MEALS. LYNTON 3 MILES. S£, D£.

RATES

Normal Bed & Breakfast rate per person **(single room)**	
PRICE RANGE	CATEGORY
Under £35	S£
£36-£45	S££
£46-£55	S£££
Over £55	S££££

Normal Bed & Breakfast rate per person **(sharing double/twin room)**	
PRICE RANGE	CATEGORY
Under £35	D£
£36-£45	D££
£46-£55	D£££
Over £55	D££££

This is meant as an indication only and does not show prices for Special Breaks, Weekends, etc. Guests are therefore advised to verify all prices on enquiring or booking.

BLUE BALL INN (on facing page)

16 BEDROOMS, ALL WITH PRIVATE BATHROOM. ALL BEDROOMS NON-SMOKING. FREE HOUSE WITH REAL ALE. CHILDREN AND PETS WELCOME. BAR AND RESTAURANT MEALS. LYNTON 2 MILES. S£££, D££.

Blue Ball Inn
formerly The Exmoor Sandpiper Inn

is a romantic Coaching Inn dating in part back to the 13th century, with low ceilings, blackened beams, stone fireplaces and a timeless atmosphere of unspoilt old world charm. Offering visitors great food and drink, a warm welcome and a high standard of accommodation.

The inn is set in an imposing position on a hilltop on Exmoor in North Devon, a few hundred yards from the sea, and high above the twin villages of Lynmouth and Lynton, in an area of oustanding beauty.

The spectacular scenery and endless views attract visitors and hikers from all over the world.

We have 16 en suite bedrooms, comfortable sofas in the bar and lounge areas, and five fireplaces, including a 13th century inglenook. Our extensive menus include local produce wherever possible, such as locally reared meat, amd locally caught game and fish, like Lynmouth Bay lobster; specials are featured daily. We also have a great choice of good wines, available by the bottle or the glass, and a selection of locally brewed beers, some produced specially for us.

Stay with us to relax, or to follow one of the seven circular walks through stunning countryside that start from the Inn. Horse riding for experienced riders or complete novices can be arranged.

Plenty of parking. Dogs (no charge), children and walkers are very welcome!

Blue Ball Inn formerly The Exmoor Sandpiper Inn
Countisbury, Lynmouth, Devon EX35 6NE
01598 741263
www.BlueBallinn.com • www.exmoorsandpiper.com

The Foxhunters Inn

West Down, Near Ilfracombe EX34 8NU

- *300 year-old coaching Inn conveniently situated for beaches and country walks.*
- *Serving good local food.*
- *En suite accommodation.*
- *Pets allowed in bar areas and beer garden, may stay in accommodation by prior arrangement. Water bowls provided.*

Tel: 01271 863757 • Fax: 01271 879313
www.foxhuntersinn.co.uk

8 BEDROOMS, ALL WITH PRIVATE BATHROOM. ALL BEDROOMS NON-SMOKING. CHILDREN AND PETS WELCOME. BAR AND RESTAURANT MEALS. ILFRACOMBE 4 MILES.

The Dolphin Inn

Kingston, Near Kingsbridge, Devon TQ7 4QE
Tel & Fax: 01548 810314

www.dolphin-inn.co.uk

Hidden away amidst the leafy lanes and high hedges of the South Hams with the thatched cottages of a tranquil village as near neighbours, this is a gem of a retreat far removed from the hustle and bustle of urban life. Tubs and hanging baskets of colourful blooms greet the visitor's entrance into an ambience of time-honoured hospitality. Sit in the inglenook with a glass of one's fancy and enjoy excellent home-cooked food served seven days a week. Why not stay for a few days? Pretty Wonwell Beach is nearby and there are lovely walks by the River Erme. Three en suite bedrooms are available offering full Bed and Breakfast with colour television and coffee-making facilities.

3 BEDROOMS, ALL WITH PRIVATE BATHROOM. ALL BEDROOMS NON-SMOKING.
PUNCH TAVERNS HOUSE WITH REAL ALE. CHILDREN WELCOME. BAR LUNCHES, RESTAURANT EVENINGS ONLY.
DESIGNATED COVERED SMOKING AREA. KINGSBRIDGE 10 MILES. S££, D£.

RISING SUN HOTEL & RESTAURANT (on facing page)

ALL BEDROOMS WITH PRIVATE SHOWER/BATHROOM. BAR AND RESTAURANT MEALS.
BARNSTAPLE 20 MILES, MINEHEAD 17.

Dating back to the 14th Century, the Rising Sun Hotel is an historic smugglers' Inn nestled in the picturesque harbour of Lynmouth. Over the years it has been gently transformed into an elegant harbourside hotel, whilst retaining its character and charm, with oak panelled dining room and bar, crooked corridors and delightful rooms.

Boasting superior service, comfortable surroundings and fine cuisine combined with truly magnificent views of the harbour and Exmoor coastline, the Rising Sun offers warmth, friendliness and a personal touch whilst providing the highest standards.

All our individually furnished bedrooms are comfortably appointed and possess a charm and individuality seldom found in modern hotels. Most have views over the harbour, assuring guests of an unforgettable experience.

Our restaurant provides an intimate and relaxed ambience. Incorporating the season's produce, maintaining quality and freshness, your meal will reach the highest standards of presentation, taste and creativity.

Rising Sun Hotel & Restaurant
Harbourside, Lynmouth
Devon EX35 6EG
Tel: 01598 753223
Fax: 01598 753480
e-mail: reception@risingsunlynmouth.co.uk
www.specialplace.co.uk

The Anchor Inn

Fore Street, Beer, Near Seaton, Devon EX12 3ET
Tel: 01297 203 86 • www.anchorinn-beer.com

Visitors can expect a high standard of hospitality at The Anchor Inn, which has a specialist seafood restaurant and friendly staff. 8 en suite bedrooms provide all modern facilities, each overlooking the unspoilt East Devon fishing village. Why not curl up beside the bar's open log fire in winter or relax in the clifftop beer garden during the summer months?

The Trout & Tipple

Julie and Shaun invite you to The Trout & Tipple, a quiet pub just a mile outside Tavistock on the A386, with a keen following for its real ale (CAMRA Listed), real food and real welcome. It is a family-friendly pub - children are welcome - with a games room, patio area, dining room and a large car park. Pets welcome. Traditional pub fare is served, with trout from the Tavistock Trout Fishery featuring on the menu; Sunday roasts are very popular. Holiday cottage available -details on request.

Parkwood Road, Tavistock Devon PL19 0JS
Tel: 01822 618886   www.troutandtipple.co.uk

NO ACCOMMODATION. FREE HOUSE WITH REAL ALE. CHILDREN AND PETS WELCOME.
BAR AND RESTAURANT MEALS. NON-SMOKING AREAS. PLYMOUTH 13 MILES.

Pet-Friendly
Pubs, Inns & Hotels
on pages 174-182
Please note that these establishments may not feature in the main section of this book

Dorset

Gloucestershire

RATES   S – SINGLE ROOM rate   D – Sharing DOUBLE/TWIN ROOM

S£ D£ =Under £35   S££ D££ =£36-£45   S£££ D£££ =£46-£55   S££££ D££££ =Over £55

This is meant as an indication only and does not show prices for Special Breaks, Weekends, etc.
Guests are therefore advised to verify all prices on enquiring or booking.

Old Manse House

Victoria Street, Bourton-on-the-Water, Gloucestershire GL54 2BX
Tel: 01451 820082 •Fax: 01451 810381• www.oldmansehotel.com

Ideally set in the centre of the Costwold village of Bourton-on-the-Water is this pretty country country hotel, restaurant and pub. Real ales, fine wines and specialty cream teas and coffees are available. For a romantic getaway, book the four-poster room. All bedrooms are en suite, with a unique ambience, and full English breakfast is included in the room rate.

The Roo Bar

Clifton Down Station, Whiteladies Road, Bristol, Gloucestershire BS8 2PN
Tel: 0117 9237204

Just a short distance from the city centre, this Aussie theme pub is predominantly a sports bar with a number of screens showing live sporting fixtures. Other facilities include two American pool tables, a well stocked bar and an imaginative menu of pub favourites.

The White Hart Inn

Lower Maudlin Street, Bristol, Gloucestershire BS1 2LU
Tel: 01179 268747 • Fax: 01179 291709

An authentic, old-fashioned city centre pub offering freshly ground coffee, comfortable leather sofas and quiet background music, as well as a good choice of refreshments and a food menu of traditional favourites - home-made beefburgers are a speciality.

The Bay Horse

1 Lewins Mead, Bristol, Gloucestershire BS1 2LJ • Tel: 01179 258287

Conveniently situated in Bristol's city centre, this drinking and dining venue offers tasty meals, plus fine wines and real ales. There is karaoke every Friday and facilities include a non-smoking area and a large screen TV.

THE STAR INN

Rhodyate Hill, Congresbury, Bristol, Gloucestershire BS49 5AJ
Tel: 01934 833441

A Listed building with low ceilings, cosy recesses and oak beams. The food is of a very high standard and diners can enjoy their meal in the spacious conservatory, or in the beer garden (weather permitting). Children are welcome at this establishment.

The Bridge Inn

North End Road, Yatton, Bristol, Gloucestershire BS49 4AU
Tel: 01934 839100 • Fax: 01934 839149

The Bridge Inn offers entertainment such as quiz nights and pool competitions and is the only pub in the area to screen live sporting fixtures. Real and cask ales are available and there is a range of lunchtime meal deals. Why not spend a romantic weekend in one of the two special suites, each with a double Jacuzzi and DVD player.

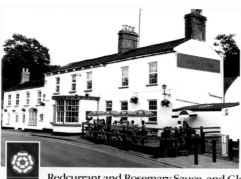

THE FOUNTAIN
INN & LODGE

Parkend, Royal Forest of Dean, Gloucestershire GL15 4JD

Traditional village inn, well known locally for its excellent meals and real ales. A Forest Fayre menu offers such delicious main courses as Lamb Shank In Redcurrant and Rosemary Sauce, and Gloucester Sausage in Onion Gravy, together with a large selection of curries, vegetarian dishes, and other daily specials.

Centrally situated in one of England's foremost wooded areas, the inn makes an ideal base for sightseeing, or for exploring some of the many peaceful forest walks nearby.

All bedrooms (including one specially adapted for the less able) are en suite, decorated and furnished to an excellent standard, and have television and tea/coffee making facilities. Various half-board breaks are available throughout the year.

Tel: 01594 562189 • Fax: 01594 564438
e-mail: thefountaininn@aol.com • www.thefountaininnandlodge.com

8 BEDROOMS, ALL WITH PRIVATE BATHROOM. ALL BEDROOMS NON-SMOKING. FREE HOUSE WITH REAL ALE. CHILDREN AND PETS WELCOME. BAR AND RESTAURANT MEALS. DESIGNATED COVERED SMOKING AREA. LYDNEY 4 MILES. S££, D£.

THE CLOSE HOTEL
Long Street, Tetbury, Gloucestershire GL8 8AQ
Tel: 01666 502 272 • 01666 504 401 • www.theclose-hotel.com
This remarkable hotel stands second-to-none in terms of 16th century elegance, and enjoys a flawless reputation for atmosphere and comfort. There is a stylish restaurant offering a superb dining experience, and a well maintained garden with central fountain. All rooms are en suite; for an extra touch of luxury two have antique four-poster beds.

The Bell Hotel
52 Church Street, Tewkesbury, Gloucestershire GL20 5SA
Tel: 01684 293 293 • Fax: 01684 295 938 • www.thebell-hotel.co.uk
The Bell enjoys a great location in the heart of medieval Tewkesbury. Its restaurant, The Priory, serves up pub favourites and a Sunday Carvery. The surrounding area has much historic architecture as well as modern shopping amenities. Rooms are en suite, with colour TV, ironing equipment, direct-dial telephone and coffee making facilities.

Somerset

The Woolpack
2 Warminster Road, Beckington, Bath, Somerset BA11 6SP
Tel: 01373 831 244 • Fax: 01373 831 223 • www.woolpackhotel.com
Beckington was renowned for its wool production in the Middle Ages - hence this historic inn's name. Today the ground floor boasts an impressive split-level bar and two dining areas serving quick snacks, while for something more substantial the Oak and Garden Rooms are available. Accommodation is in 11 en suite bedrooms.

The Assembly Inn
16-17 Alfred Street, Bath, Somerset BA1 2QU
Tel: 01225 333639
This busy pub is popular with students, office workers and shoppers, and offers a good choice of beers, real ales and pub snacks in a traditional setting.

The Boathouse
Newbridge Road, Bath, Somerset BA1 3NB • Tel: 01225 482584
The Boathouse is situated by the water's edge and features a well maintained garden, perfect for outdoors enthusiasts in summer months. The interior layout is contemporary and open-plan in style, and the bar stocks a good choice of wines, beers, and real ales. The main menu offers a variety of home cooked meals and pub snacks are available.

The George Inn
Mill Lane, Bathampton, Bath, Somerset BA2 6TR • Tel: 01225 425079
Situated near the River Avon and the Tennyson Avon Canal, the George affords delightful views of the river and boats. The interior is traditional in style, with oak beams, open fires and little alcoves, nooks and crannies. The menu offers a good range of specials including fish dishes, and the Sunday roast lunch is deservedly popular.

The Wheatsheaf

Combe Hay, Bath, Somerset BA2 7EG • Tel: 01225 833504

Wooden beams and a roaring log fire contribute to this pub's traditional atmosphere. With large terraced gardens, lawns and stunning landscape views, it has an excellent reputation for serving delicious meals, ideal for the whole family. Facilities include a large beer garden, and BBQs are held during summer months.

The Dustan House Inn

8-10 Love Lane, Burnham on Sea, Somerset TA8 1EU • Tel: 01278 784343

Situated just a short walk from the centre of Burnham on Sea, this friendly inn serves delicious food freshly prepared by the highly skilled chef, and the bar is stocked with a good selection of real ales, beers and wines. Accommodation is in six en suite bedrooms with modern facilities. Children and dogs are welcome.

THE LION
at Pennard

Glastonbury Road, West Pennard, Glastonbury BA6 8NH
Tel: 01458 832941 • e-mail: d.pennard@btconnect.com

The Lion at Pennard is a 15th century coaching inn, complete with deep inglenook fireplaces, flagstone floors and oak beams. Accommodation is available in seven comfortable en suite bedrooms, making this an ideal base for visiting the many places of interest in the area, including the historic towns of Wells and Glastonbury.

Delicious bar and restaurant meals can be enjoyed each lunchtime and evening. Children are welcome; high chairs are available if required. The lounge bar offers an excellent range of refreshments, and visitors will receive a warm welcome from the friendly staff — and perhaps from the resident ghost who is believed to sit there! Bed and breakfast rates are most reasonable. Dogs welcome.

7 BEDROOMS, ALL WITH PRIVATE BATHROOM. ALL BEDROOMS NON-SMOKING. REAL ALE.
CHILDREN AND DOGS WELCOME. BAR AND RESTAURANT MEALS. GLASTONBURY 3 MILES. D££.

The Bristol Inn

Chapel Hill, Clevedon, Somerset BS21 7NL • Tel: 01275 872073

There's never a dull day here at the Bristol Inn, located in the heart of Clevedon village and just a short walk from the beach. A wide choice of beers and ales is available behind the bar, and there is regular entertainment, with live music/disco on Fridays. Facilities include a pool table, dart board, terraced seating and a snug area.

Wiltshire

The White Hart Inn

Ford, Chippenham, Wiltshire SN14 8RP
Tel: 01249 782213 • Fax: 01249 783075 • www.marstonsinns.co.uk

This inn's reputation for serving up culinary delights precedes it, with a full à la carte menu and bar snacks available. The original Dr Dolittle film was filmed here and it has since been used for TV adverts. Accommodation is in 11 rooms, all en suite, with wifi, flat screen TV with Freeview, hairdryer and tea/coffee making facilities.

The Green Dragon

26 High Street, Market Lavington, Devizes, Wiltshire SN10 4AG
Tel: 01380 813235 • www.greendragonlavington.co.uk

An award-winning inn, with a good selection of real ales, lagers, beers and fine wines, and a superior reputation for food and accommodation. Facilities include an enclosed garden with a pets section and a BBQ area.

The Wheatsheaf Inn

Oaksey, Near Malmesbury, Wiltshire SN16 9TB
Tel: 01666 577348 • Fax: 01666 575067

Set in this beautifully rural part of Wiltshire, the inn retains traditional features such as low beams and a chimney with carved crosses on it to fend off witches. Facilities include a skittle alley, quoits, bar skittles and dominoes, and there is a popular restaurant. A holiday cottage is available to rent - telephone for further details.

THE GEORGE INN *The Square, Mere, Wiltshire BA12 6DR* WCT/AA ★★★

A detour from the busy A303 to sample the relaxing properties of this 16th century inn is heartily recommended. A popular feature of a picturesque little town now enabled to revert to its previous tranquil way of life, the inn, known until recently as the Talbot Hotel, has a stirring history and a just as stirring rebirth, having been carefully refurbished with original features such as exposed beams, stone walls and flagstone floors maintaining its age-old character. In 1651 King Charles II, fleeing from the forces of Oliver Cromwell, dined here en route to safety and exile that lasted eight years. Today, relaxation and the provision of quality chef-inspired fare is the order of the day and handsome overnight en suite accommodation is available at reasonable rates.

una.white@btconnect.com • www.thegeorgeinnmere.co.uk

Tel: 01747 860427
Fax: 01747 861978

7 BEDROOMS, ALL WITH PRIVATE BATHROOM. HALL & WOODHOUSE HOUSE WITH REAL ALE.
CHILDREN WELCOME. BAR AND RESTAURANT MEALS. NON-SMOKING AREAS. SHAFTESBURY 7 MILES. S£, D££.

London (Central & Greater)

Tower Bridge   photo courtesy PDPhoto.org

The Royal Oak

Longbridge Road, Barking, Greater London IG11 8UF
Tel: 020 8507 1600 • www.pub-explorer.com/gtlondon/pub/royaloakbarking.htm
An friendly establishment offering a wide range of draught beers and real ales, plus DJs
every Friday and Saturday and regular 70s/80s nights. There are BBQs in summer and
live sporting fixtures shown on plasma screens. Over 18s only.

The Coach & Horses

Burnhill Road, Beckenham, Greater London BR3 3LA • Tel: 0208 6509142
www.pub-explorer.com/gtlondon/pub/coach&horsesbeckenham.htm
A small likeable pub situated near the beautiful gardens in Kelsey Park. It offers a great
selection of draught beers including Guinness and Strongbow, as well as regular and
guest real ales. Patio area; wheelchair access throughout.

The Blue Anchor

Bridgen Road, Bexley, Greater London DA5 1JE

Tel: 01322 523582 • www.pub-explorer.com/gtlondon/pub/blueanchorbexley.htm

Good honest beer, real ales and hearty meals are served in this lively pub restaurant. Facilities include an IT box, jukebox, dartboard and pool tables. plus live sporting fixtures shown on plasma screens for that all-important match. A children's menu is available.

The George

74 Bexley High Street, Bexley, Greater London DA5 1AJ

Tel: 01322 523843 • www.pub-explorer.com/gtlondon/pub/georgebexley.htm

A sports bar with a wide selection of cold draught beers and real ales. There's no chance of missing out on an important match, with live sporting fixtures shown on the numerous TVs positioned throughout. Enjoy the quality burger menu and live monthly entertainment. Outdoor eating area available.

The King's Arms

156 The Broadway, Bexleyheath, Greater London DA6 7DW • Tel: 020 8303 1173

All on one level, this busy pub serves breakfast, steaks and a variety of other meals throughout the day. The bar stocks a wide selection of draught beers and fine wines. Regular events include a Monday dart team, Tuesday quiz night and Wednesday poker league. Wifi throughout and a jukebox.

The Yacht

Long Lane, Bexleyheath, Greater London DA7 5AE

Tel: 020 8303 4889 • www.pub-explorer.com/gtlondon/pub/yachtbexleyheath.htm

Customers can expect faultless service at this Steak and Ale house, famed for its airy, open plan arrangement as well as the mouth-watering dishes on offer. Children can amuse themselves in the designated play area while you relax over a fine wine or real ale. Activities include pool night on Tuesday, quiz night on Thursday and two pool tables.

The Crown

155 Bromley Common, Bromley, Greater London BR2 9RJ

Tel: 020 8460 1472 • www.pub-explorer.com/gtlondon/pub/crownbromley.htm

Situated just 2.5 miles from Bromley town centre, the pub restaurant's contemporary interior attracts a large variety of customers in search of a chilled pint, ale, coffee, or food from the full à la carte menu; children's menu also available. Facilities include a quiet area, patio area, baby changing facilities and disabled toilet.

Freelands Tavern

31 Freelands Road, Bromley, Greater London BR1 3HZ • Tel: 020 8464 2296 •

www.pub-explorer.com/gtlondon/pub/freelandstavernbromley.htm

The Freelands is known for its firm commitment to sport, screening all major fixtures on impressive plasma screens. A great selection of hot and cold food is also available – toasties, jacket potatoes, rib-eye steaks etc. The bar serves a good selection of draught beers, wines and real ales. A popular beer garden is perfect during the summer months.

Shortlands Tavern

Station Road, Shortlands, Bromley, Greater London BR2 0EY
Tel: 020 8460 2770 • www.pub-explorer.com/gtlondon/pub/shortlandstavern.htm

Shortlands is situated next to the railway station and overlooks the platform. Relax in the beer garden over one of the carefully selected wines, beers and ales, or get involved in one of the pub's weekly activities – quiz night, speed pool, or dart. Sports fans can watch that all-important match on the big screen. Children are welcome (till 7pm).

Spaniard's Inn

Spaniards Road, Hampstead Heath, London NW3 7JJ • Tel: 020 8731 6571

Known affectionately as 'The Spaniard's', this legendary pub stands just round the corner from Hampstead Heath. There is a genuine pub atmosphere, with historic artefacts everywhere you look – all proof that the inn was indeed a hideout for a number of highwaymen including Dick Turpin himself! The bar is always well stocked, and the burgers, soups and meat platters are a 'must try'!

The Rose & Crown

55 High Street, Wimbledon Village, London SW19 5BA
Tel: 020 8947 4713 • Fax: 020 8947 4994 • www.roseandcrownwimbledon.co.uk

Situated within walking distance of the All England Lawn Tennis Club, Wimbledon Theatre and Wimbledon Common, with good train links to central London. Enjoy a cold draught beer or real ale at the friendly bar, dine in comfort inside the snug restaurant or in the airy, heated courtyard. 13 en suite rooms, all with plasma Sky TV, and coffee/tea making facilities.

The Windmill on The Common

Clapham, London SW4 9DE
Tel: 020 8673 4578 • www.windmillclapham.co.uk

A friendly public house blended with a modern hotel, the newly furbished Windmill serves a good range of beers and lagers on tap and boasts a new à la carte menu, with specials changed daily. Accommodation is in 29 luxurious en suite air-conditioned rooms, equipped with king-size beds, plasma screens, freeview TV, fresh milk and wifi.

The White Swan

Riverside, Twickenham, Greater London TW1 3DN • Tel: 020 8892 2166

Quietly situated by the Thames is this wooden floored, L-shaped bar, the walls of which are decorated with rugby memorabilia. On busy days, the BBQs on the outdoor terrace are very popular, making it an ideal spot for a cold pint and light bite after a riverside walk. Regular live music and sporting fixtures; bar menu available. Children welcome.

White Cross Hotel Pub

Riverside (Off Waterlane), Richmond, Surrey TW9 1TH
Tel: 020 8940 6844 • www.youngs.co.uk

Patrons are eagerly encouraged to sample the wide range of Young's award-winning real ales, wines and food. This is the ideal place to go for a cool pint and light bite after the rugby. Facilities include wifi, a beer garden, and log fire

Wheatsheaf Pub

6 Stoney Street, Borough, London SE1 9AA • Tel: 020 7407 7242 • www.pubs.com

Young's have refurbished this tiny market pub and stocked it with a good range of beer. Its two-bar concept has been retained - public and saloon. Enjoy a tipple by the crackling log fire on a winter evening. It is within walking distance of Clink Prison Museum and Southwark Cathedral, as well as the new art-house clubs by London Bridge station.

Westminster Arms

Storey's Gate, Westminster, London SW1P 3AT • Tel: 020 7222 8520 • www.pubs.com

Take a trip to the heart of Westminster for one of many real ales stocked at this pub-restaurant-wine bar. This three-floored establishment, located near to Big Ben, is popular with local office workers. Snacks are available at the bar but for a more relaxing meal, dine upstairs or outside at street level and people watch. The pub is reputedly haunted by the ghost of a boy who died in the Great Fire of London!

The Warrington Hotel

93 Warrington Crescent, Maida Vale, London W9 1EH
Tel: 020 7286 2929 • www.gordonramsay.com/thewarrington

When this pub became an object of chef Gordon Ramsay's affections, there was no turning back … and who would want to? Guests are of course guaranteed a feast from the exquisite menu. For lovers of fine wine and beer (and a casual dress code) – make the Warrington your next destination.

Guards at Buckingham Palace

Viaduct Tavern

126 Newgate St, Holborn, London EC1A 7AA
Tel: 020 7600 1863 • www.pubs.com

Located opposite the Holborn Viaduct, this little corner pub offers customers a relaxed environment away from the hustle and bustle in which to enjoy real ales, wines and beers. Sandwiches are available Monday to Friday at lunchtimes. Original features date back to 1869, the year Queen Victoria opened the Holborn Viaduct. Nearest Tube – St Paul's.

Trafalgar Tavern

Park Row, Greenwich, London SE10 9NW • Tel: 020 8858 2909

Charles Dickens, William Gladstone and several senior Members of Parliament frequented this Regency-style drinking house in the mid-19th century. After a major refurbishment the Trafalgar is now much more than just a pub, with a restaurant, bar and banqueting suites. Bar snacks are available at the Duncan Bar and mouth-watering fish dishes are a 'must try' in the Collingwood Restaurant.

Town of Ramsgate

62 Wapping High Street, London E1W 2PN • Tel: 020 7481 8000 • www.pubs.com

This narrow pub has a murky but interesting past. Situated next to the Wapping Old Stairs, an alleyway that leads down to the riverside, one can quite believe that convicts would use the narrow path as an escape route all those years ago. Now it is a welcoming local for East Londoners and visiting friends.

Tower of London

THE TOTTENHAM

6 Oxford Street, London W1D 1AN • Tel: 020 7636 7201 • www.pubs.com

Believe it or not, the Tottenham is the last remaining pub out of the 38 that used to exist on London's famous Oxford Street, and was built by the famous Baker Brothers. This is the ideal place to go after work for a quick pint to unwind from the day's stresses.

Tom Cribb

36 Panton Street, London SW1Y 4EA • Tel: 020 7839 3801 • www.pubs.com

Come to Tom Cribb's and spot performers from the local 'luvvie' hinterland. Named after Tom Cribb himself, the bare-knuckle fighter turned publican, this traditional Piccadilly pub serves a good range of beers and ales on tap. Come in for a hearty meal, light sandwich or jacket potato. Facilities include TV and air-conditioning.

The Tipperary

66 Fleet St, London EC4Y 1HT
Tel: 020 75836470 • www.pubs.com

Situated on London's Fleet Street, this authentic Irish pub serves Guinness with a smile. The pub is open all day, with wheelchair access and real ales!

Star Tavern

6 Belgrave Mews West, Belgravia, London SW1X 8HT
Tel: 020 7235 3019 • www.pubs.com

Lunchtimes are busy at the Star Tavern - proof that great food is served here! It is situated in Belgravia, the area bordering Knightsbridge, and offers a taste of the 'real' London. CAMRA Pub of the Year 2005/6, with a beautiful new dining room upstairs and real ales.

St Stephen's Tavern Pub

10 Bridge Street, Westminster, London SW1A 2JR
Tel: 020 7925 2286 • www.pubs.com

A jewel in London's political district, this friendly pub's customers are a mixture of office workers from the Houses of Parliament and tourists. There is a little bar at the back and a mezzanine floor area for functions.

Spread Eagle

71 Wandsworth High Street, Wandsworth, London SW18 4LB
Tel: 020 8877 9809 • www.pubs.com

One of Young's original and bigger public houses, situated in the centre of Wandsworth town, serving a wide range of draught beer and real ales. Facilities include Sky TV, a big screen for live sporting fixtures, a dartboard and fruit machines. Food is served throughout the day. Nearest station is East Putney.

Seven Stars Pub

53 Carey Street, Holborn, London WC2A 2JB
Tel: 020 7242 8521 • www.pubs.com

The Seven Stars is a very special pub, having survived the Great Fire of London. Despite the odd adjustment here and there, the pub remains very much as it was. It has a narrow bar leading to a cosy snug at the back, real ale, an open fire, wooden settles and a few tables and chairs.

The Ship

116 Wardour Street, Soho, London W1F 0TT
Tel: 020 7437 8446 • www.pubs.com

Come and immerse yourself in the creative atmosphere of this Soho pub - Wardour Street is the centre of the TV and film-making industry and The Ship is popular with many in the business. The bar is well stocked with Fuller's draught and real ales.

The Salisbury

90 St Martin's Lane, London WC2N 4AP • Tel: 020 7836 5863 • www.pubs.com

One of only two pubs in the UK to be awarded the Beautiful Beer Platinum Award, The Salisbury has been well maintained over the years. It offers six well-kept real ales, and a highly imaginative menu for the perfect pub lunch or early dinner. It is conveniently situated just a stone's throw from Theatreland and Covent Garden.

RED LION PUB

48 Parliament Street, Whitehall, London SW1A 2NH
Tel: 020 7930 5826 • www.pubs.com

Situated between the House of Commons and Downing Street, The Red Lion is popular with politicians, civil servants and journalists. An upstairs dining room and cellar bar provide extra space for busy times of day.

Richard I Pub

52 Royal Hill, Greenwich, London SE10 8RT
Tel: 020 8692 2996 • www.pubs.com

Located on a quiet back street in Greenwich is this charming 1920s conversion, offering two bar areas, and a beer garden for BBQs, al fresco drinking and dining in summer months. The menu ranges from ciabattas and sandwiches to big burgers, jacket potatoes , fish and chips and chilli con carne. Children are welcome till 8.30pm.

Pet-Friendly
Pubs, Inns & Hotels

on pages 174-182
Please note that these establishments may not feature in the main section of this book

Red Lion

Crown Passage, Off Pall Mall, St James's, London SW1Y 6PP
Tel: 020 7930 4141 • www.pubs.com

This pub can get very busy but it is deservedly popular. The bar stocks a good selection of whiskies and beers, and for a light bite, filling sandwiches at affordable prices. The surrounding are area retains a genial Dickensian ambience, particularly as it is still gas lit!

The Queen's Larder

1 Queen's Square, Bloomsbury, London WC1N 3AR
Tel: 020 7837 5627 • www.pubs.com

The Queen's Larder has associations with King George III and his wife, Queen Charlotte, and today offers real ale and a good selection of draught beers. For a quiet pint in a great area of London, take the Piccadilly Line and get off at Russell Square.

Punch Bowl Pub

41 Farm St, Mayfair, London W1J 5RP
Tel: 020 7493 6841 • www.pubs.com

The Punch Bowl is a enjoyably understated little pub situated in London's Mayfair. Simple decorations outside and inside mean there's no risk of pretentiousness or over-priced drinks and food - ideal for time out whether working or sightseeing.

The Prospect Of Whitby

57 Wapping Wall, Wapping, London E1W 3SJ • Tel: 020 7481 1095 • www.pubs.com

Children and dogs are welcome at this famous London pub. Sip real ale by the open fire and dine in style in the pub's restaurant.It gets very crowded here on weekends so come early and nab yourself a picnic bench! Tower Bridge, The Wapping Project and St Katherine's Docks are all nearby.

PRINCESS LOUISE

208 High Holborn, Holborn, London WC1V 7BW • Tel: 020 7405 8816

Dickens wrote about the Inns of Chancery in his novel Great Expectations - one of these quiet pubs still in existence is the Princess Louise. At this delightful spot both food and drink are on a par in terms of excellence. The recent refurbishment has brought about several welcome additions: cosy cubicles, draught and bottled beers, and an extensive range of dishes at realistic prices. Closed Sundays.

Prince Alfred Pub

5a Formosa Street, Maida Vale, London W9 1EE • Tel: 020 7286 3287

This is one of the last remaining authentic Victorian pubs, Grade II Listed, and now in competition with Gordon Ramsay's Warrington, round the corner. So class conscious were the Victorians that pubs such as this were built compartmentally, each of the five bars having a separate entrance. At the back, there is a dining room with a bar.

Berkshire

The Sun In The Wood

Stoney Lane, Ashmore Green, Berkshire RG18 9HF
Tel: 01635 42377 • www.suninthewood.co.uk

Countryside pub restaurant situated in beautiful Berkshire, near Newbury.
Facilities include a nine-hole crazy golf-pitch, a small conservatory area,
a decked terrace with old fashioned street lights, and a child-free section.

The Bell at Boxford

Lambourn Road, Boxford, Berkshire RG20 8DD
Tel: 01488 608721 • www.bellatboxford.com

Award-winning countryside inn, standing in the peaceful Lambourne Valley
countryside and commended for its regularly changing menu. The Bell offers
free wireless internet throughout. Each of the 10 en suite bedrooms has
direct-dial telephone, trouser press, hairdryer and coffee/tea tray.

The Swan

High Street, East Isley, Newbury, Berkshire RG20 7LF
Tel: 01635 281238 • www.theswaneastilsley.co.uk

After an extensive renovation, the historic inn just 10 miles north of Newbury boasts five
single or double en suite bedrooms and a luxurious bridal suite. Room rates include full
English breakfast, colour TV, coffee/tea making facilities, internet access and hairdryer.
Children have a special play area located in the beer garden. Parking available.

THE WEE WAIF

Old Bath Road, Charvil, Near Reading, Berkshire RG10 9RJ
Tel: 0118 9440 066 • Fax: 0118 9691 525 • www.weewaif.tablesir.com

Situated in the tranquil village of Charvil, with easy access to Reading, London and
Heathrow. The restaurant is open seven days a week and features a daily-changing
specials board. A range of accommodation will suit all requirements, with Sky TV, en
suite bath and shower, and extra linen. Newbury racecourse is just 40 minutes away.

Buckinghamshire

Ye Old Jug

Lower Rd, Hardwick, Aylesbury, Buckinghamshire HP22 4DZ
Tel: 01296 641303 • www.yeoldejug.com

With easy links to nearby London and Oxford, this delightful establishment offers a wide variety of activities throughout the year. Facilities include a beer garden, indoor and outdoor function areas, a large plasma TV and wifi access throughout.

The Saracen's Head Inn

38 Whielden Street, Amersham Old Town, Bucks HP7 0HU
Tel: 01494 721958 • www.thesaracensheadinn.com

Hear the chilling tale of the two ghosts who reputedly roam this 17th century inn at night. With an outdoor area for BBQs and an open log fire in the bar area, this charming English pub provides a unique ambience. Lunch and evening meals are available in the restaurant and accommodation includes single, double and family size rooms.

Gatehanger's Freehouse

Lower End, Ashendon, Aylesbury, Bucks HP18 0HE
Tel: 01296 651296 • www.gatehangers.co.uk

This traditional countryside inn is situated just a short drive from Aylesbury village, with neighbouring Oxford close by. The five en suite bedrooms offer coffee and tea making facilities, and the restaurant serves home-cooked food made from local produce, with bar snacks available Friday lunchtimes and a weekly Sunday roast.

BROUGHTON HOTEL

Broughton, Milton Keynes, Buckinghamshire MK10 9AA
Tel: 01908 667726 Fax: 01908 604844 www.thebroughton.com

Ideal for a stopover and fully equipped with amenities to keep the whole family entertained, with five plasma screens, a beer garden/patio area and children's play area. The restaurant provides an extensive menu, with a Wednesday curry night. All rooms have recently been decorated and have an en suite shower and bath.

Hampshire

The Swan Hotel
High Street, Alton, Hampshire GU34 1AT
Tel: 01420 83777 • Fax: 01420 87975 • www.swanalton.com
Jane Austen afficionados can enjoy a visit to her cottage in nearby Chawton, now a museum displaying her life's work. With a lavishly decorated interior and well furnished bedrooms, The Swan is an ideal place to stay. Thes 36 en suite rooms have colour TV, tea/coffee making facilities, and wifi throughout.

The Hen & Chicken
Upper Froyle, Alton, Hampshire GU34 4JH
Tel: 01420 22115 • www.henandchicken.co.uk
On the A31, a friendly establishment where children are welcome, with their own special play area. Traditional features include an inglenook fireplace and a large beer garden, and the food menu includes classic dishes and pub meals. The well stocked bar offers wines, beers and real ales.

The Danebury Hotel
2 High Street, Andover, Hampshire SP10 1NX
Tel: 01264 323 332 • 01264 335 440 • www.thedaneburyhotel.com
Just a short drive from Stonehenge is this luxurious town house hotel which dates back centuries. These days it is the place to go at weekends, with a busy disco and late bar. Relax after lunch or dinner with a glass of wine on one of the soft leather sofas in the The Market Bar. Guests can expect high quality accommodation with amenities including satellite TV.

RATES   S – SINGLE ROOM rate   D – Sharing DOUBLE/TWIN ROOM

S£ D£ =Under £35   S££ D££ =£36-£45   S£££ D£££ =£46-£55   S££££ D££££ =Over £55

This is meant as an indication only and does not show prices for Special Breaks, Weekends, etc.
Guests are therefore advised to verify all prices on enquiring or booking.

The Raven Hotel
Station Road, Hook, Hampshire RG27 9HS
Tel: 01256 762 541 • Fax: 01256 768 677 • www.theraven-hotel.com

Former guests of this elegant hotel include Enid Blyton and Edward VIII. It enjoys a convenient position half an hour away from Windsor Castle, the New Forest, Bird World, Ascot, Windsor and Newbury racecourses, and Reading Football Club. Accommodation is in 38 en suite bedrooms, each with modern facilities.

The Farmhouse Inn Lodge
Burrfields Road, Portsmouth, Hampshire PO3 5HH
Tel: 023 92650510 • www.farmhouseinnlodge.com

Five miles from Goodwood Racecourse and Portsmouth's historic Dockyard, this is an ideal place to relax - and best of all – play, with an 18-hole golf course and driving range nearby. Guests can dine in the lounge or outside on the patio. Two honeymoon suites and 74 other rooms are available, as well as executive and leisure suites.

Cricketers Inn
Curdridge, Southampton, Hampshire SO32 2BH • Tel: 01489 784420

At the Cricketers, the social calendar is crammed with exciting events and is constantly being updated. As well as entertainment, this friendly establishment offers an impressive selection of beers, carefully selected wines and real ales. The staff provide friendly service in the restaurant, where the food is first class.

THE GROSVENOR HOTEL
23 High Street, Stockbridge, Hampshire SO20 6EU
Tel: 01264 810 606 • Fax01264 810 747 • www.thegrosvenor-hotel.com

This Georgian-style hotel is situated between the cathedral cities of Winchester and Salisbury. Dishes featuring local produce such as the chef's speciality Test Trout are on the menu in The Tom Cannon Restaurant. The wood panelled Bankside Bar also offers an à la carte menu and a range of snacks. A new wing provides accommodation with modern facilities.

RATES

Normal Bed & Breakfast rate per person **(single room)**		Normal Bed & Breakfast rate per person **(sharing double/twin room)**	
PRICE RANGE	CATEGORY	PRICE RANGE	CATEGORY
Under £35	S£	Under £35	D£
£36-£45	S££	£36-£45	D££
£46-£55	S£££	£46-£55	D£££
Over £55	S££££	Over £55	D££££

This is meant as an indication only and does not show prices for Special Breaks, Weekends, etc. Guests are therefore advised to verify all prices on enquiring or booking.

New Forest Ponies. Picture courtesy of Hampshire County Council

Isle of Wight

The Fountain Inn

High Street, Cowes, Isle of Wight PO31 7AW
Tel: 01983 292 397 • 01983 299 554 • www.fountaininn-cowes.com

This Isle of Wight 'must-see' is famous in yachting circles as home to the Royal Yacht Club. It offers panoramic views of the harbour and shoreline, an early-bird buffet breakfast and a famous 'kilo of mussels' dinner. 20 en suite rooms all have direct-dial telephone, TV, hairdryer, trouser press and CD player.

Ryde Castle

Esplanade, Ryde, Isle of Wight PO33 1JA
Tel: 01983 563 755 • Fax: 01983 566 906 • www.rydecastle.co.uk

Visiting the Ryde Castle is like diving into a history textbook. This regal looking establishment has been a hospital and army HQ during both World Wars. Indulge in a pre-dinner drink and then dine in style in the brasserie. 18 en suite bedrooms have all modern facilities. Blackgang Chine and Fantasy Theme Park are nearby.

The Isle of Wight has several award-winning beaches, including Blue Flag winners, all of which are managed and maintained to the highest standard. Sandown, Shanklin and Ryde offer all the traditional delights; or head for Compton Bay where surfers brave the waves, fossil hunters admire the casts of dinosaur footprints at low tide, kitesurfers leap and soar across the sea and paragliders hurl themselves off the cliffs

Newport is the commercial centre of the Island with many famous high street stores and plenty of places to eat and drink. Ryde has a lovely Victorian Arcade lined with shops selling books and antiques. Cowes is great for sailing garb and Godshill is a treasure chest for the craft enthusiast. Lovers of fine food will enjoy the weekly farmers' markets selling home-grown produce and also the Garlic Festival held annually in August.

The Island's diverse terrain makes it an ideal landscape for walkers and cyclists of all ages and abilities. Pony trekking and beach rides are also popular holiday pursuits and the Island's superb golf courses, beautiful scenery and temperate climate combine to make it the perfect choice for a golfing break.

Kent

The Orchard Spot

Spot Lane, Otham, Maidstone, Kent ME15 8SE
Tel: 01622 861802 • Fax: 01622 861801 • www.theorchardspot.co.uk
The interior is stylish and contemporary, and it enjoys a spectacular location amongst open fields in this beautiful area of Kent. The restaurant serves delicious food at affordable prices and the bar stocks an impressive choice of real ales and beers.

The Flagship

115 Snargate St Dover, Kent CT17 9DA
Tel: 01322 862087
A stylish Kentish establishment offering menu classics such as seafood and mature steaks, plus carefully selected wines, guest beers and real ales. Parking available.

Kings Arms Hotel

Market Square, Westerham, Kent TN16 1AN
Tel: 01959 562 990 • Fax: 01959 561 240 • www.the-kingsarms.com
Take full advantage of the sales at Blue Water Shopping Centre, which is located only 20 minutes away. Enjoy some chilled entertainment over a light lunch or early evening tipple in The Conservatory, light and airy for summer relaxation. All rooms are en suite, with satellite TV and music centre.

Pet-Friendly
Pubs, Inns & Hotels
on pages 174-182
Please note that these establishments may not feature in the main section of this book

Oxfordshire

Surrey

The Ely

London Road (A30), Blackwater, Camberley, Surrey GU17 9LJ
Tel: 01252 860 444 • Fax: 01252 878 265 • www.theely.com

The Ely is simply perfect for motorists looking for a cosy and traditional stopover on the M3. With an alluring redbrick exterior and outdoor terrace, passersby can't resist taking a break for refreshment. Children are well catered for in the hotel's restaurant and outdoor play area. Rooms are en suite, with TV, hairdryer and trouser press facilities.

THE COMPASSES INN

Station Road, Gomshall, Surrey GU5 9LA
Tel: 01483 202506

This attractive inn was once known as the 'God Encompasses' but through time and mispronunciation is now simply known as the 'Compasses'. Known for its appetising selection of home-cooked dishes and supporting local Surrey Hills Brewery, this friendly hostelry has a warm ambience accentuated by its exposed oak beams and horse brasses. There is good home-cooked food in the bar and the restaurant; à la carte menu available in the evenings. Situated beneath the North Downs, there is a popular beer garden through which runs the Tillingbourne Stream. *A tranquil port of call amidst delightful countryside.*

2 BEDROOMS, ALL WITH PRIVATE BATHROOM. REAL ALES. CHILDREN WELCOME, PETS ALLOWED IN BAR ONLY. BAR AND RESTAURANT MEALS. GUILDFORD 6 MILES. ££££ PER ROOM PER NIGHT.

Family-Friendly
Pubs, Inns & Hotels
See the Supplement on pages 183-186 for establishments which really welcome children

The Hurtwood Inn Hotel

Set at the heart of the picturesque village of Peaslake, in the beautiful Surrey Hills, this family-run, privately owned hotel has an enviable reputation for the individuality and quality of its cuisine and hospitality

Ideally placed to explore some of England's finest countryside, such as Leith Tower Hill, South of England's highest point with breathtaking views, the National Trust properties of Polesden Lacey and Clandon Park, and nearby the historic county town of Guildford.

Hotel of the Year • Millenium South East England Tourist Board Award 2000 (under 50 bedrooms)

21 tastefully furnished en suite bedrooms. 'Oscars' Restaurant with superb local reputation, serving modern and traditional cuisine in the intimate dining room.

Hurtwood Inn Hotel, Walking Bottom, Peaslake, Near Guildford, Surrey GU5 9RR
Tel: 01306 730851 • Fax: 01306 731390
e-mail: sales@hurtwoodinnhotel.com • www.hurtwoodinnhotel.com

21 BEDROOMS, ALL WITH PRIVATE FACILITIES. ALL BEDROOMS NON SMOKING. FREE HOUSE WITH REAL ALE. CHILDREN AND PETS WELCOME. BAR AND RESTAURANT MEALS. S££££, D££££.

White Cross Hotel Pub
Riverside (Off Waterlane), Richmond, Surrey TW9 1TH
Tel: 020 8940 6844 • www.youngs.co.uk
Patrons are eagerly encouraged to sample the wide range of Young's award-winning real ales, wines and food. This is the ideal place to go for a cool pint and light bite after the rugby. Facilities include wifi, a beer garden, and log fire.

Visit the FHG website

www.holidayguides.com

for details of the wide choice of accommodation

featured in the full range of FHG titles

East Sussex

THE ANCHOR INN

Anchor Lane, Barcombe, Near Lewes, East Sussex BN8 5BS

This delightful retreat hidden away on the west bank of the River Ouse is a great favourite. Peacefully situated in a beautiful part of leafy Sussex, the inn has an interesting history. It was built in 1790 and catered primarily for bargees whose horse-drawn barges plied between Newhaven and nearby Slaugham. After the decline of river traffic, locals continued to use the inn until the innkeeper was unwary enough to be caught smuggling in 1895: the licence was rescinded and not regained until 1963. At one with the unspoilt daily life of the river, this is a lovely place to escape to and boating can be arranged. The inn itself has great character and offers comfortable accommodation at reasonable rates.

Tel: 01273 400414 • Fax: 01273 401029 • www.anchorinnandboating.co.uk

3 BEDROOMS, ALL WITH PRIVATE BATHROOM. ALL BEDROOMS NON-SMOKING. FREE HOUSE WITH REAL ALE. BAR AND RESTAURANT MEALS. NON-SMOKING AREAS. LEWES 4 MILES. S£££, D££.

The Druid's Head

9 Brighton Place, Brighton, East Sussex BN1 1HJ
Tel: 01273 325490

A popular Sussex Coast pub and diner with an unpretentious atmosphere. Some of the outside brickwork dates all the way back to 1510, with sash windows and other period features. The cuisine is varied and of a very high standard, and beers and ales are well kept.

The Franklin Tavern

158 Lewes Road, Brighton, East Sussex BN2 3LF
Tel: 01273 602995 • Fax: 01273 698535

The pub is close to Brighton University and is popular with family and friends visiting students. Food and drinks are reasonably priced, and live sporting fixtures are shown on large plasma screens.

The Buccaneer

10 Compton Street, Eastbourne, East Sussex BN21 4BW • Tel: 01323 732 829

Located in the heart of theatreland and popular with patrons for a pre- or post-theatre tipple, this majestic building was built in the style of the Pavilion at Brighton. It offers a good selection of hand-pulled real ales and other refreshments. Pub food is served every day from a varied menu, and Sunday lunch is particularly popular.

The Farm@Friday Street

Friday Street, Langney, Eastbourne, East Sussex BN23 8AP
Tel: 01323 766049 • www.whitingandhammond.co.uk

After an extensive refurbishment, oak beams, stone-flagged floors, authentic log fires and leather sofas create a welcoming pub atmosphere. Food and drink is reasonably priced, with the emphasis on fresh local produce wherever possible.

THE WHEEL INN

Heathfield Road, Burwash Weald, Etchingham, East Sussex TN19 7LA
Tel: 01435 882758 • Fax: 01435 883625

The Wheel Inn is situated in an area of outstanding natural beauty and offers a good choice of lagers, beers, spirits and mixers. This free house stocks its own British cask conditioned real ales. Facilities include a pool table and dart board.

The Swan Mountain

Lewes Road, Forest Row, East Sussex RH18 5ER • Tel: 01342 822318

The Swan Mountain is well worth seeking out. The interior is very cosy, with open log fires, low-beamed ceilings and a snug – all the traditional features one hopes to find in a friendly family pub. Other delightful features include a restaurant area and a sun terrace for outdoor dining in summer months.

The Roebuck

Wych Cross, Forest Row, East Sussex RH18 5JL
Tel: 01342 823 811 • Fax: 01342 824 790 • www.theroebuck.co.uk

Winnie the Pooh fans may remember hearing about Forest Row as it borders Royal Ashdown Forest, where the famous bear lived! Summers are delightful at the Roebuck with its outdoor patio and restaurants. Accommodation is in 30 en suite bedrooms, all with modern facilities. Brighton and Royal Tunbridge Wells are a short drive away.

The White Hart

Winchelsea Road, Guestling, Near Hastings, East Sussex TN35 4LW
Tel: 01424 813187

The White Hart is a Beefeater pub in an Grade II Listed building with a country house atmosphere. Log fires and traditional furnishings and fittings create a charming olde worlde ambience, and the bar is stocked with a good variety of beers, lagers, ales and fine wines. Children are welcome at this establishment, and there is a large beer garden.

The Blind Busker

75- 7 Church Road, Hove, East Sussex BN3 2BB • Tel: 01273 749110

Great staff and a stylish interior with comfy seating areas, rugs, drapes and a modern colour scheme are the basis of this friendly pub's first class reputation. Food is very popular here and Sunday lunches on the outdoor decking area are a firm favourite, with a choice of burgers, swordfish and a variety of other tasty delights.

The Green Man

Lewes Road, Ringmer, East Sussex BN8 5NA
Tel: 01273 812422 • www.greenmanringmer.co.uk

The new decked patio area makes outdoor dining a real treat here at the Green Man in Ringmer. The restaurant has a reputation for good service and even better food - the Sunday Carvery is especially popular and is a great excuse for a family day out. The bar is stocked with a varied selection of beers, lagers, real ales and fine wines.

The White Horse

Marine Drive, Rottingdean, East Sussex BN2 7HR
Tel: 01273 300 301 • Fax: 01273 308 716 • www.whitehorsehotelrottingdean.com

Enjoy a scrumptious lunch outside on the decked patio/ terrace and afterwards take a short trip along the coast to explore the many delights of Brighton. The 19 newly decorated bedrooms have exquisite sea views, en suite facilities and all mod cons.

West Sussex

RATES　S – SINGLE ROOM rate　　D – Sharing DOUBLE/TWIN ROOM

S£ D£ =Under £35　　S££ D££ =£36-£45　　S£££ D£££ =£46-£55　　S££££ D££££ =Over £55

This is meant as an indication only and does not show prices for Special Breaks, Weekends, etc.
Guests are therefore advised to verify all prices on enquiring or booking.

Bedfordshire

The Bull

259 London Road, Bedford, Bedfordshire MK42 0PX
Tel: 01234 355719 • www.myspace.com/thebullbedford

The Bull with its mock Tudor exterior offers an extensive selection of weekly activities, including a quiz night, pool tournament, and Thursday night curry club. With a wide range of pub snacks, food deals and drinks offers, wifi, and live sport on plasma screens, there is something for everyone. Children and dogs are welcome in the outdoor area.

The Castle

Newham Street, Bedford, Bedfordshire MK40 3JR • Tel: 01234 353295

Located in a popular area of Bedford, The Castle dates back 200 years, and is a perfect place for post-work get-togethers over an ale or fine wine. Home-made, hearty meals are of great value and size – Punjabi dishes are on the menu Fridays and Saturdays for the more adventurous palate. B&B accommodation is available in one single and three twin rooms.

The Fox and Hounds

178 Goldington Road, Bedford, Bedfordshire MK40 3EB • Tel: 01234 353993

Enjoy the drinks offers and entertainment in this modern-style pub, situated close to the University. Weekly activities include pool, karaoke (and bingo if no football on TV!). Pub snacks and main meals are available as well as a children's menu.

The Pheasant

300 Kimbolton Road, Bedford, Bedfordshire MK41 8YR
Tel: 01234 409301 • www.pub-explorer.com/beds/pub/pheasantbedford.htm

A Bedfordshire pub for all the family, with live sport shown on two large-screen TVs, a children's play area, pool table and dart board. The lunchtime menu offers freshly prepared pub favourites accompanied by teas, coffees, real ales and fine wines. In summer months the beer garden is popular with locals and visitors alike.

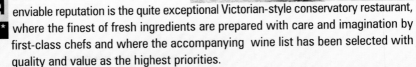

The Boater

Icknield Way, Luton, Bedfordshire LU3 2JR
Tel: **01582 575191**• www.pub-explorer.com/beds/pub/boaterluton.htm
Visitors can expect good quality ales at this friendly Cask Marque accredited pub. Located
on Icknield Way with local businesses nearby, The Boater is the ideal place for important
business lunches. Regular events include Monday quiz nights and poker on a Wednesday,
with BBQs and pool on the outdoor decked area during summer months.

The Biscot Mill

310 Biscot Road, Luton, Bedfordshire LU3 1AS
Tel: **01582 572363** • www.pub-explorer.com/beds/pub/biscotmill.htm
This community-based pub welcomes visitors and boasts features such as combo
booth/TV seating and a wine wall. It is predominantly a restaurant, offering a
Hungry Horse menu (children's menu also available). A wide range of draught beers
and ales is on offer. Facilities include a beer garden, and patio area,

THE Globe INN

Globe Lane, Stoke Road, Old Linslade,
Leighton Buzzard, Bedfordshire LU7 7TA

★ Canal-side location with access over own bridge.
★ Beer garden with outdoor eating facilities
★ Bar/Lounge open all day, every day
★ Children welcome ★ Children's play area
★ Dining area with non-smoking section
★ Excellent choice of food served 12 noon to 9pm daily
★ Cask Marque Accredited 2005
★ Booking Highly Recommended
Tel: 01525 373338 • Fax: 01525 850551

NO ACCOMMODATION. GREENE KING HOUSE WITH REAL ALE. CHILDREN WELCOME.
BAR AND RESTAURANT MEALS. LUTON 11 MILES.

The Old Coach House

12 Market Street, Potton, Bedfordshire, SG19 2NP
Tel: **01767 260221** • www.pottoncoachhouse.co.uk • info@pottoncoachhouse.co.uk
This privately owned inn has undergone several refurbishments, yet still preserves its
original character. Accommodation is in 12 bedrooms, each with en suite shower or
bath, colour TV and complimentary beverage tray. Food is home-cooked and is served
lunchtimes and evenings. The Old Coach House is strictly non-smoking.

THE FOX & HOUNDS

High Street, Riseley, Bedfordshire MK44 1DT
Tel: **01234 708240** • www.pub-explorer.com/beds/pub/foxandhoundsriseley.htm
Pretty flowerpots hang on the white-washed walls of this delightful Cask Marque
accredited pub. Guests can enjoy a mouth-watering steak, accompanied by one of the
pub's cask ales, fine wines or malt whiskies. Soak up the traditional atmosphere in the oak-
beamed dining rooms and library room, and relax in the beer garden in summer months.

THE BLACK HORSE

Ireland, Near Shefford, Bedfordshire SG17 5QL

Tel: 01462 811398 • Fax : 01462 817238 • www.blackhorseireland.com

A beautifully presented traditional inn with several points of interest nearby, including National Trust sites, the Shuttleworth Collection and a variety of golf courses. All rooms have an en suite shower facility, and each has a unique garden entrance. Colour TV, fridge and coffee/tea making facilities are provideds. No pets or smoking allowed.

The Three Cranes

High Street, Turvey, Bedfordshire MK43 8EP

Tel: 01234 881305 • Fax: 01234 881156 • www.threecranes-turvey.com

The Three Cranes has three en suite bedrooms, all with a comforting country feel, plus TV, coffee/tea tray and iron. The local butcher is quite literally next door, a firm guarantee that all meat dishes are fresh and locally sourced. Children welcome. Listed in the Good Beer Guide and Cask Marque accredited.

Queens Head Hotel

Rushden Road, Milton Ernest, Bedfordshire MK44 1RU

Tel: 01234 822 412 • 01234 822 337 • www.queenshead-miltonernest.com

Milton Ernest was a favourite haunt of the American musician, Glenn Miller, and pre-war the village was home to 30 different trades and crafts. Today the Queens Head serves hearty meals at affordable prices and the bar boasts a range of real ales. All rooms are en suite, with colour TV and hot beverage making facilities.

The Anchor

397 Goldington Road, Bedford, Bedfordshire MK41 0DS

Tel: 01234 353606 • www.pub-explorer.com/beds/pub/anchorbedford.htm

The Anchor has recently undergone a complete refurbishment and now serves good value Giant Plate meals, real ale and carefully selected wines in new and relaxing surroundings. There is a beautiful lounge conservatory in which to spend a Sunday afternoon, and during the summer months, the whole family can enjoy the beer garden and bouncy castle.

The White Hart

22 - 24 Market Square, Biggleswade, Bedfordshire SG18 8AR

Tel: 01767 314219 • www.pub-explorer.com/beds/pub/whitehartbiggleswade.htm

As the second oldest building in Biggleswade, The White Hart has seen many people come and go - particularly with a closing time of 1am on Friday and Saturday! With deals on food and drink as well as wifi access throughout, this finger-on-the-pulse pub's modernity is enhanced by an in-house DJ at weekends. Car parking available.

The Yorkshire Grey

140 London Road, Biggleswade, Bedfordshire SG18 8EL • Tel: 01767 313222

www.pub-explorer.com/beds/pub/yorkshiregreybiggleswade.htm

Another homely Giant Plate pub boasting an exclusive coffee lounge seating area. It provides extra cool draught pumps and a regular rotation of drinks and meal deals, as well as weekly entertainment - music and general knowledge quizzes, karaoke nights and live sport shown on three plasma screens. Children welcome. Car park available.

Cambridgeshire

THE ANCHOR INN

Sutton Gault, Near Ely, Cambridgeshire CB6 2BD
Tel: 01353 778537 • Fax: 01353 776180
e-mail: anchorinn@popmail.bta.com
www.anchor-inn-restaurant.co.uk

The 17th Century Anchor Inn offers modern British cuisine with an emphasis on seasonal and traditional ingredients; superb wine list. We have four guest bedrooms offering a variety of accommodation to suit every need. The Anchor is ideally situated for exploring East Anglia; it is only 7 miles from Ely and is less than half an hour from Cambridge. Newmarket and its racecourse are within easy reach.

4 BEDROOMS, ALL WITH PRIVATE BATHROOM. ALL BEDROOMS NON-SMOKING. FREE HOUSE WITH REAL ALE. CHILDREN WELCOME. ELY 6 MILES. S££££, D££.

The Boathouse

14 Chesterton Road, Cambridge, Cambridgeshire CB4 3AX • Tel: 01223 460905
Pleasant, waterside establishment set in beautiful Cambridgeshire surroundings, serving real ales, Continental lagers, soft drinks and Costa coffee. Amenities include a games room, plasma screen TVs, a pool table, beer garden, and a varied food menu offering English, Thai, Mexican and Italian cuisine.

The Fox

Gladeside Bar Hill, Cambridge, Cambridgeshire CB3 8DY • Tel: 01954 780305
Bar Hill's pride and joy – a stylish, well maintained venue with a sociable layout. Children are welcome, and amenities include an outdoor children's play area, pool table and jukebox.

Milton Arms

205 Milton Road, Cambridge, Cambridgeshire CB4 1XG • Tel: 01223 505012

Situated in a residential area north of Cambridge, the Milton Arms is a member of the Hungry Horse hospitality scheme, with a large dining area and a peaceful lounge area with comfy furniture. Amenities include wifi access, a new outdoor children's play area, a sports bar with a pool table, flat screen TVs, and a beer garden and alfresco dining area.

The Red Lion

33 High Street, Grantchester, Cambridgeshire CB3 9NF • Tel: 01223 840121

Traditional, thatched pub located in an idyllic area by the river in Grantchester; a path in the garden leads to the tranquil River Cam, an ideal after-dinner walk. The first-class menu offers seafood and game dishes, plus a vegetarian option, and there is also a children's menu.

The George

High Street, Spaldwick, Huntingdon, Cambridgeshire PE28 0TD • Tel: 01480 890293

This pub's high street setting means that it is a firm favourite with locals as well as passers by. The mixture of olde world and contemporary is well balanced - spotlights in the ceiling and leather sofas, yet open fires for winter cosiness. The restaurant has a great reputation, with a choice of Mediterranean, New World and English cuisine.

The Waggon & Horses

39 High Street, Milton, Cambridgeshire CB4 6DF • Tel: 01223 860313

Listed in *The Good Beer Guide* is this prominent mock-Tudor style venue with an interesting preoccupation with hats and pictures - and an impressive collection of both! In the beer garden are swings, a slide and chickens too! Regular features include bar billiards, a quiz night, balti night, a dart board and piano.

CROWN AND PUNCHBOWL INN

High Street, Horningsea, Cambridgeshire CB5 9JG
Tel: 01223 860643 • Fax: 01223 441814

This charming, recently restored 17th century inn is situated in the unspoilt riverside village of Horningsea which lies four miles north-east of Cambridge. Not only is it an ideal stopover for visitors to the City but also for those touring East Anglia. In the old bars, with their exposed timbers and inglenook fireplace, open fires during the winter months add to the warm welcome. The inn has an enviable reputation for its food, offering excellent quality restaurant meals. In the evenings, candlelight adds to the ambience. The double and twin en suite bedrooms, recently refurbished to a very high standard, all have digital television, telephone, wifi connection and tea and coffee-making facilities and guests may look forward to a hearty English breakfast in the morning.

e-mail: info@thecrownandpunchbowl.co.uk • www.thecrownandpunchbowl.co.uk

5 BEDROOMS, ALL WITH PRIVATE BATHROOM. FREE HOUSE WITH REAL ALE. CHILDREN WELCOME. RESTAURANT MEALS. TOTALLY NON-SMOKING. CAMBRIDGE 4 MILES. S£££, D££££.

The Halcyon

Atherstone Avenue, Peterborough, Cambridgeshire PE3 9TT
Tel: 01733 263801

After an extensive makeover, The Halcyon offers a Hungry Horse food menu – affordable and varied! Regular activities include live bands and a poker night, and there is a dart board, pool table and a smoking shelter with TV installed!

The Harrier

184 Gunthorpe Road, Peterborough, Cambridgeshire PE4 7DS
Tel: 01733 575362 • Fax: 01733 575364

A modern family pub, a member of the Hungry Horse group, where the menu is a major attraction. The staff are particularly helpful and work tirelessly behind the well stocked bar. Facilities include a pool table, big screen TV and decked chill-out area for adults.

Palmerston Arms

82 Oundle Road, Peterborough, Cambridgeshire PE2 9PA
Tel: 01733 565865 • www.palmerston-arms.co.uk

'The Palmy' is an olde world pub steeped in traditional pub values. Behind the bar is a selection of good quality real ales, draught ciders and perry, direct from the cask. When hunger strikes, try a Cornish pasty or freshly made pie.

THE WOODMAN

Thorpe Wood, Peterborough, Cambridgeshire PE3 6SQ • Tel: 01733 267601

Situated in the Longthorpe area is this golfing themed inn, furnished with suede and leather seats and sofas. Early breakfast is available for dedicated golfers and the regular food menu is available from noon onwards. Wifi access, TV, pool table, large beer garden and patio area.

Essex

Hertfordshire

The Mitre Inn

58 High Street, Barnet, Hertfordshire EN5 5SJ

Tel: 020 8449 6582 • www.pub-explorer.com/herts/pub/mitrebarnet.htm

This dog-friendly (on leads!) pub is positioned on Barnet's popular and busy high street.
The bar stocks a wide range of draught beers, real ales and cocktails (to order), all of which
can be enjoyed in the bar, living area or restaurant. Live sporting fixtures on plasma screens.

The Duke Of York

Ganwick Corner, Barnet Road, Barnet, Hertfordshire EN5 4SG

Tel: 0208 4490297 • www.pub-explorer.com/herts/pub/dukeofyorkbarnet.htm

Superbly refurbished gastro bar and dining room, with easy access to
Barnet High Street and Arkley countryside. It offers draught beers and regularly
changing guest ales at the bar, and an imaginative menu in the restaurant.

THE SUN HOTEL

Sun Street, Hitchin, Hertfordshire SG5 1AF

Tel: 01462 432 092 • Fax: 01462 431 488 • www.sunhotel-hitchin.com

The Sun, with its delightful interior, is situated in Hitchin and dates back to the
16th century. Enjoy an excellent meal in the hotel's restaurant, which features dishes
from around the world as well as traditional English cuisine. Real ales and fine wines
are also available. 32 en suite bedrooms have wifi, CD player and colour TV.

The Valiant Trooper

Trooper Road, Aldbury, Tring, Hertfordshire HP23 5RW

Tel: 01442 851203 • www.valianttrooper.co.uk/

This Valiant Trooper offers many traditional feaures such as beamed ceilings, an
inglenook fireplace, exposed brickwork, and a woodburning stove. The converted barn
at the rear (now a restaurant) completes this beautifully positioned establishment.

Norfolk

THE OLD HALL INN is an old world character freehouse/restaurant situated on the coast road between Cromer and Great Yarmouth. It is in the middle of the village and just five minutes' walk from one of the best beaches along the Norfolk coast. There are six letting rooms, three of which are en suite, all have tea/coffee making facilities and TV.

THE OLD HALL INN
Sea Palling
NR12 0TZ
Tel: 01692 598323
Fax: 01692 598822

There is a non-smoking à la carte restaurant and bar meals are also available.

Wireless internet available.

Well behaved children and pets are welcome.

Prices start at £35 for a single room, inclusive of full English breakfast, and £50 for a double room (two persons) per night.

6 BEDROOMS, 3 WITH PRIVATE BATHROOM. ALL BEDROOMS NON-SMOKING. FREE HOUSE WITH REAL ALE. CHILDREN AND PETS WELCOME. BAR AND RESTAURANT MEALS. DESIGNATED COVERED SMOKING AREA. HAPPISBURGH 4 MILES. S£, D£££.

RATES

Normal Bed & Breakfast rate per person
(single room)

PRICE RANGE	CATEGORY
Under £35	S£
£36-£45	S££
£46-£55	S£££
Over £55	S££££

Normal Bed & Breakfast rate per person
(sharing double/twin room)

PRICE RANGE	CATEGORY
Under £35	D£
£36-£45	D££
£46-£55	D£££
Over £55	D££££

This is meant as an indication only and does not show prices for Special Breaks, Weekends, etc. Guests are therefore advised to verify all prices on enquiring or booking.

FREE or REDUCED RATE entry to Holiday Visits and Attractions –

see our **READERS' OFFER VOUCHERS** on pages 187-218

Suffolk

THE WORKS £3 00

The Mill Inn
Market Cross Place, Aldeburgh, Suffolk IP15 5BJ
Tel: 01728 452563 • www.themillinnaldeburgh.com
On the sea front at Aldeburgh, this popular pub provides comfortable accommodation and easy access to the beach, as well as to shopping amenities, cinema and theatre. Drop in for a delicious bar snack or a glass of real ale. Rooms have colour TV, tea/coffee tray, and hairdryer.

THE BROME GRANGE HOTEL
Norwich Road, Brome, Near Eye, Suffolk IP23 8AP
Tel: 01379 870456 • www.bromegrange.co.uk • bromegrange@fastnet.co.uk
Set amid the Suffolk countryside, The Grange boasts 22 ground floor en suite rooms, all with views of the beautiful hotel gardens. Single, double, twin or family size rooms are available. The stylish Knight's Restaurant serves à la carte international and English dishes with produce from the hotel's own organic free-range farm.

The Beehive
The Street, Horringer, Bury St Edmunds, Suffolk IP29 5SN • Tel: 01284 735260
This beautiful pub boasts an award-winning restaurant serving fresh, home-made dishes prepared from local ingredients. The building has exposed flint walls, and inside is traditional in style, with pine furniture, oak beams and a number of charming little nooks and crannies.

The Dog & Partridge
29 Crown Street, Bury St Edmunds, Suffolk IP33 1QU • Tel: 01284 764792
Put your overnight bag down at the adjacent inn and pop in to the pub next door for a nightcap. Drink and dine in peace, play some pool, watch the football highlights, or simply pull up a pew outside in either of the two courtyards. Accommodation is nine non-smoking bedrooms. Wifi hotspot available.

THE GROSVENOR

25/31 Ranelagh Road, Felixstowe, Suffolk IP11 7HA • Tel: 01394 284137

This authentic public house has retained most of its original features, and the interior includes comfortable lounges, a pool room and a bar area. Live sporting fixtures are shown on a large screen TV, with a jukebox and a dart board for patrons' enjoyment.

The Huntsman & Hound

Stone Street, Spexhall, Halesworth, Suffolk IP19 0RN • Tel: 01986 781341

Traditional 15th century Inn close to the Suffolk coast, with the Norfolk Broads just a short drive away. Stay in one of three bedrooms, each en suite, with colour TV and coffee/tea making facilities. Enjoy a pint of real ale in the bar area and some freshly home-cooked food. Pets welcome by arrangement.

The Thrasher

Nacton Road, Ipswich, Suffolk IP3 9RZ • Tel: 01473 723355

Having undergone a major refurbishment, the pub is now a focal point of the local community. The stylish interior is elegantly decorated, with impressive LCD TV screens in the restaurant's seating area. The cuisine is particularly popular, with something for everyone on the imaginative menu.

The Crown

9 Ipswich Road, Claydon, Ipswich, Suffolk IP6 0AA
Tel: 01473 830289 • Fax: 01473 832986

Standing proudly in Claydon village on the edge of Ipswich, this attractive establishment offers a good value Hungry Horse menu. Oak beams and a beer garden make this an attractive spot to stop off for refreshment on a day out.

The Bell Inn

Walberswick, Southwold, Suffolk IP18 6TN
Tel: 01502 723109 • Fax: 01502 722728

Those who really do want to escape from the 21st century will find the perfect retreat in this delightful little Suffolk village at the mouth of the River Blyth – just miles of peaceful, unspoilt beaches and surrounding countryside, as tranquil and uncluttered as it was centuries ago. A recommended halt in this tiny paradise is the 600-year-old Bell Inn with its stone floors, oak beams, high wooden settles and crackling log fires creating an atmosphere that lulls one into forgetfulness of modern life and its pressures. Traditional pub fare is on hand, with the emphasis on freshly caught local fish, and overnight accommodation takes the form of pleasantly furnished bedrooms with views over sea or river.

e-mail: bellinn@btinternet.com • www.blythweb.co.uk/bellinn

6 BEDROOMS, ALL WITH PRIVATE BATHROOM. FREE HOUSE WITH REAL ALE. BAR AND RESTAURANT MEALS. SOUTHWOLD 1 MILE.

The Man On The Moon

86 Palmcroft Road, Ipswich, Suffolk IP1 6QX • Tel: 01473 464182

A cosmopolitan pub venue situated in a residential area on the outskirts of Ipswich. Sport is taken seriously here and many of the regulars come to watch the live sporting fixtures on the large screen TV. The bar is stocked with a good choice of real ales, beers and wines, and food is served throughout the week at affordable prices.

THE PUNCH & JUDY

41 Grafton Street, Ipswich, Suffolk IP1 1UZ • Tel: 01473 210979

The Punch & Judy is a converted Two For One family pub situated in the Cardinal Entertainment Park. This very modern establishment is the ideal place to relax over a pint of real ale or beer. Delicious meals are available and children can amuse themselves at the indoor Fun House, while parents relax.

The Angel Hotel

Lavenham, Market Place, Lavenham, Suffolk CO10 9QZ

Tel: 01787 247388 • Fax : 01787 248344 • www.theangelhotel.com

15th Century medieval inn positioned in the heart of Lavenham, with 8 en suite bedrooms and a sitting room in which residents can relax and enjoy a tipple. The hotel has a reputation for a good selection of bar ales and good food.

THE BIRD IN HAND

The Street, Beck Row, Near Mildenhall, Suffolk IP28 8ES

Tel: 01638 713247 • Fax: 01638 711207

This popular venue comprises a restaurant, bar area and pool room. A wide range of dishes is available from an extensive menu, plus a good selection of wines, beers and other refreshments. Accommodation is in 57 en suite bedrooms with modern facilities including tea/coffee-making equipment and wifi throughout.

The Bell Hotel

Market Hill, Clare, Sudbury, Suffolk CO10 8NN

Tel: 01787 277741 • Fax: 01787 278474

This Listed building has many traditional features, including a Tudor-style frontage, and offers a warm welcome to visitors to this ancient town. The conservatory menu features a wide range of home-made dishes, all served with fresh vegetables. 16 en suite bedrooms have all modern facilities, including tea/coffee-making equipment.

The White Horse

The Street, Easton, Woodbridge, Suffolk IP13 0ED

Tel: 01728 746456 • Fax: 01728 747492

The award-winning White Horse is an exceptionally pretty inn situated in Easton, with many picturesque walks nearby, as well as water mills and castles to visit. Freshly prepared food is served all day throughout the week, and children are welcome.

Derbyshire

Ye Olde Cheshire Cheese Inn

How Lane, Castleton, Hope Valley S33 8WJ
Telephone: 01433 620330 • Fax: 01433 621847

• Situated in the heart of the picturesque Peak District, our traditional 17th century family-run Inn is full of character, and is ideally situated to explore the natural beauty of the area.

• The Inn offers a wide selection of draught beers and has an excellent reputation for award-winning cask ales and traditional home-cooked food.

• All 10 bedrooms are en suite, comfortably furnished, and have colour television and tea/coffee facilities.

• There is a large car park adjacent to the Inn, and you are assured of a warm and friendly welcome from Karen and John and their helpful staff.

www.cheshirecheeseinn.co.uk
e-mail: info@cheshirecheeseinn.co.uk

10 BEDROOMS, ALL EN SUITE. ALL BEDROOMS NON-SMOKING. FREE HOUSE WITH REAL ALE.
BAR AND RESTAURANT MEALS. HATHERSAGE 5 MILES. S£, D£.

THE LITTLE JOHN INN
Station Road, Hathersage
Hope Valley
Derbyshire S32 1DD

This handsome stone building which dates from the 19th century is popular with locals and visitors alike. It has won awards for its ale and carries a good selection of refreshments. This is just the place for a relaxing drink or meal after a day walking on the high moors. Home-cooked food is served in the bar, and there are two plasma screen TVs. The pub is mainly non-smoking. Accommodation is available in five en suite rooms and two charming cottages

Owner Stephanie Bushell offers all guests a warm welcome.

Tel: 01433 650225 • • Fax: 01433 659831

5 BEDROOMS, ALL WITH PRIVAE BATHROOM. TWO COTTAGES. REAL ALE. BAR MEALS.
CHILDREN AND PETS WELCOME. BAKEWELL 8 MILES.

Herefordshire

RED LION HOTEL
Bredwardine, Herefordshire HR3 6BU

This 17th century former coaching inn stands in its own well-kept grounds in the centre of Bredwardine, with the Black Mountains towering to the west. The old world charm of the public rooms, enhanced by antiques, oaken beams and open fireplaces, is complemented well by the excellent modern amenities of the well prepared guest bedrooms, all individually furnished to a high degree of comfort. Enjoy home cooked evening meals using mainly local produce. A peaceful haven in the tranquil heart of England.

Tel: 01981 500 303
Fax: 01981 500 400
www.redlion-hotel.com

10 BEDROOMS, ALL WITH PRIVATE BATHROOM. FREE HOUSE WITH REAL ALE. PETS WELCOME.
BAR LUNCHES, RESTAURANT EVENINGS ONLY. NON-SMOKING AREAS. HEREFORD 11 MILES. S£££, D£££.

BASKERVILLE ARMS HOTEL
Delightfully placed in the upper reaches of the Wye Valley with the Black Mountains and Brecon Beacons on the doorstep, this comfortable retreat could not be better placed for lovers of both lush and wild unspoilt scenery. Hay-on-Wye, the 'town of books' is only 1.2 miles away with its narrow streets, antique shops and over 30 bookshops. Run by resident proprietors, June, David and Rhyddian, the hotel provides tasty, home-cooked food in bar and restaurant, using the best local produce. With so many pursuits to enjoy in the area, this little hotel is a fine holiday base and well-appointed en suite bedrooms serve the purpose excellently.

AA
★★

Clyro, Near Hay-on-Wye, Herefordshire HR3 5RZ
Tel: 01497 820670 *See website for Special Rate Breaks*
e-mail: info@baskervillearms.co.uk • www.baskervillearms.co.uk

13 BEDROOMS, ALL WITH PRIVATE BATHROOM. ALL BEDROOMS NON-SMOKING. FREE HOUSE WITH REAL ALE.
CHILDREN AND PETS WELCOME. BAR AND RESTAURANT MEALS. BRECON 17 MILES. S££, D££.

The New Inn

Market Square, Pembridge, Leominster, Herefordshire HR6 9DZ
Tel: 01544 388427

The last battle of the Wars of the Roses was fought just a few miles from here at Mortimers Cross, and the treaty which gave England's crown to the Yorkist leader is believed to have been signed in the courtroom of this fourteenth century inn. Two ghosts are said to haunt the Inn: one a girl who appears only to women; the other a red-coated soldier armed with a sword.

A varied and interesting menu is offered at most reasonable prices in the bar, which has a log fire to warm it on chillier days, and the attractive lounge area is a popular venue for cosy evening dinners.

NO ACCOMMODATION. FREE HOUSE WITH REAL ALE. CHILDREN WELCOME.
BAR AND RESTUARANT MEALS. DESIGNATED COVERED SMOKING AREA. KINGTON 6 MILES.

The Royal Hotel
Palace Pound, Ross-on-Wye, Herefordshire HR9 5HZ
Tel: 01989 565 105 • Fax: 01989 768 058 • www.theroyal-ross.com

Charles Dickens and Queen Victoria are former visitors at the eye-catching Royal Hotel. Browse through the shops in the local market town or relax at the hotel with a cream tea and scone on the Riverside Terrace. Later, sample the extensive menu, perhaps with a real ale or fine wine. Accommodation is in 42 en suite rooms, each with a truly astonishing view.

Pet-Friendly
Pubs, Inns & Hotels
on pages 174-182
Please note that these establishments may not feature in the main section of this book

Leicestershire & Rutland

Lincolnshire

THE RED LION INN   ETC ★★★★

Skegness Road, Partney, Spilsby PE23 4PG • Tel: 01790 752271

Situated at the junction of the A16/A158 at Partney.
Award-winning home-made food - extensive starters menu,
30 main courses with additional daily specials and a choice
of 22 desserts with additional daily specials. Real ales and
guest ales. 4-Star en suite accommodation (two double
rooms, one twin room). Ideally situated on the edge
of the Lincolnshire Wolds. Great for walking and
sightseeing in Lincoln, Grimsby, Boston, Skegness,
Horncastle, Alford, Gibraltar Point, The Wash, and much more.

www.redlioninnpartney.co.uk • e-mail: enquiries@redlioninnpartney.co.uk

3 BEDROOMS, ALL WITH PRIVATE BATHROOM. REAL ALE. CHILDREN OVER 10 YEARS WELCOME.
BAR AND RESTAURANT MEALS. SPILSBY 2 MILES. S£, D£.

RATES

Normal Bed & Breakfast rate per person **(single room)**		Normal Bed & Breakfast rate per person **(sharing double/twin room)**	
PRICE RANGE	CATEGORY	PRICE RANGE	CATEGORY
Under £35	S£	Under £35	D£
£36-£45	S££	£36-£45	D££
£46-£55	S£££	£46-£55	D£££
Over £55	S££££	Over £55	D££££

This is meant as an indication only and does not show prices for Special Breaks,
Weekends, etc. Guests are therefore advised to verify all prices on enquiring or booking.

Northamptonshire

THE FALCON HOTEL

Castle Ashby, Northampton, Northamptonshire NN7 1LF
Tel: 01604 696 200 • Fax: 01604 696 673 • www.falconhotel-castleashby.com
With Silverstone and Stratford-upon-Avon only a short distance away, one can be assured of an outstanding level of modern English cuisine and excellent service at The Falcon. Accommodation can be found in the hotel itself or in one of the cottages next door. Each room is en suite with a full range of modern facilities.

The Swan at Lamport

Harborough Road, Lamport, Northamptonshire NN6 9EZ
Tel: 01604 686 555 • theswanlamport@tiscali.co.uk
The Swan at Lamport is the ideal place to come on sunny days and rainy afternoons! It features a stylish interior and offers a carefully selected stock of wines and real ales. All dishes on the varied menu are prepared from fresh ingredients.

The Talbot Hotel

New Street, Oundle, Northamptonshire PE8 4EA
Tel: 01832 273 621 • Fax: 01832 274 545 • www.thetalbot-oundle.com
Much of this fine building was built from the ruins of Fotheringhay Castle, which has associations with Mary, Queen of Scots, and it is rumoured that her spirit haunts the hotel. Accommodation is in 35 uniquely designed en suite bedrooms, each with modern facilities and modem plug-in points.

Saracens Head Hotel

219 Watling Street West, Towcester, Northants NN12 6BX
Tel: 01327 350 414 • Fax: 01327 359 879 • www.saracenshead-towcester.com
This sturdy hotel dates back to the 19th century and is mentioned in Dickens' first novel, 'The Pickwick Papers'. Very popular in the town, it is renowned for wholesome meals such as fish and chips, and steaks cooked to your liking. Accommodation is in 21 en suite bedrooms. There is easy access to Towcester and Silverstone racecourses.

Nottinghamshire

The Chesterfield at Bingham
Church Street, Bingham, Nottinghamshire NG13 8AL
Tel: 01949 837342 • www.thechesterfield.co.uk
A gastro pub retaining several original features, the Chesterfield offers an imaginative menu of dishes prepared from locally sourced ingredients, and diners may eat alfresco in the delightful beer garden. For a pint of your favourite draught beer or real ale, The Chesterfield is the ideal place.

THE CHESTERFIELD ARMS
Main Road, Gedling, Nottingham, Nottinghamshire NG4 3HL • Tel: 01159 878686
Located in the peaceful village of Gedling, with pretty hanging baskets outside, this eye-catching pub is devoted to sport, with live fixtures shown on screens throughout. Food is affordably priced and entertainment includes quiz and race nights.

The Travellers Rest
Mapperley Plains, Nottingham, Nottinghamshire NG3 5RT
Tel: 0115 9264412 • Fax: 0115 9203134
This superb pub is set in rural surroundings, yet with easy access to Nottingham town centre. Chef & Brewer pubs are known for serving mouthwatering dishes at affordable prices; the speciality here is a fresh fish supper. Why not sample one of the pub's quality wines or real ales to accompany your meal?

The Fiveways
Edwards Lane, Nottingham, Nottinghamshire NG5 3HU • Tel. 0115 9265612
Edwardian-style woodcarvings enhance the traditional exterior of this old coaching house, where refreshment is reasonably priced and the choice is extensive. Facilities include a piano room, a beer garden and two smoking shelters.

The Navigation Inn

6 Wilford Street, Nottingham, Nottinghamshire NG2 1AA • Tel: 0115 9417139

Canalside city centre pub with a beautiful terraced seating area, very popular
on weekend evenings, with live music and a bubbly atmosphere.
Quality drinks and food guaranteed.

YATES'S

49 Long Row, Nottingham, Nottinghamshire NG1 6JB • Tel: 0115 947 3334

Located in the centre of Nottingham, with easy links in and out of town, this particular
branch of Yates's is very popular. The conservatory is a delightful feature, with leather
couches. Regular DJs at weekends.

The Windsor Castle

Carlton Hill, Carlton, Nottingham, Nottinghamshire NG4 1EB • Tel: 0115 9871374

Since its refurbishment two years ago, this lively pub now boasts its very own stage
and dance floor. Sport is important here, with live matches shown on the big screen,
and customers can enjoy watching the game with a pint of their favourite ale
and a tasty snack.

The Goose at Gamston

Gamston, Nottingham, Nottinghamshire NG2 6NA • Tel: 0115 9821041

The Goose is positioned in idyllic surroundings in Gamston and is an ideal family retreat, especially during summer months. The interior is elegant, with high ceilings and traditional wooden beams. The menu offers a wide range of tasty dishes, and for children (or big kids), there is ice cream!

The Chesterfield Arms

Main Road, Gedling, Nottingham, Nottinghamshire NG4 3HL • Tel: 01159 878686

Located in the peaceful village of Gedling, with pretty hanging baskets outside, this eye-catching pub is devoted to sport, with live fixtures shown on screens throughout. Food is affordably priced and entertainment includes quiz and race nights.

The Rose & Crown

Derby Road, Lenton, Nottingham, Nottinghamshire NG7 2GW • Tel: 0115 9784958

Situated in Lenton, Nottingham's student area, the Rose & Crown is a lively pub where good food is served and great company is free! Amenities include a beer garden, DJs, live music, a pool table, dart board, five TVs and a big screen for live sporting fixtures.

The Tree Tops

Plains Road, Mapperley, Nottingham, Nottinghamshire NG3 5RF
Tel: 0115 9558989 • Fax: 0115 9674031

Located just outside Nottingham in rural surroundings, and ideal for a peaceful lunchtime drink, the Tree Tops is cosy, with printed wallpaper and comfy sofas. The bar is stocked with real ales kept to a first class standard, and traditional pub food is available throughout the day.

THE THREE PONDS

Kimberley Road, Nuthall, Nottingham, Nottinghamshire NG16 1DA
Tel: 0115 9383170 • Fax: 0115 9382153

A friendly pub with an extensive menu of home-made dishes served in generous portions. The bar is stocked with a good selection of high quality real ales and draught beers. Regular activities include a popular quiz night and a poker night.

The Ferry Inn

Main Road, Wilford, Nottingham, Nottinghamshire NG11 7AA
Tel: 0115 981 1441 • Fax: 0115 982 5089

Wilford is a quaint little village with a river flowing through it, and the pub is like something out of a fairytale, with low ceilings, real inglenook fires, wood-panelled recesses and attractive hanging baskets. Chef & Brewer pubs are renowned for serving superb food made from fresh ingredients, plus a good selection of quality beers, real ales and fine wines.

Shropshire

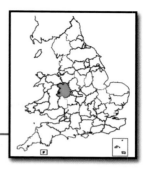

THE *Crown* COUNTRY INN

Set below the rolling hills of Wenlock Edge, the Crown Country Inn is an ideal place to stay and explore the area. This Grade II Listed Tudor inn retains many historic features, including oak beams and flagstone floors.

Here you can sample traditional ales, fine food and a warm welcome from hosts, Richard and Jane Arnold. The menu offers a tempting variety of traditional and more exotic dishes, plus daily 'specials', all freshly prepared using the finest ingredients. Accommodation is available in three large bedrooms, all en suite, with television and tea/coffee making facilities.

• *Shropshire Good Eating Awards* • *Restaurant of the Year*

www.crowncountryinn.co.uk • **info@crowncountryinn.co.uk**

**Munslow
Near Craven Arms
Shropshire SY7 9ET
Tel: 01584 841205**

3 BEDROOMS, ALL WITH PRIVATE BATHROOM. ALL BEDROOMS NON-SMOKING. FREE HOUSE WITH REAL ALE. CHILDREN WELCOME. BAR AND RESTAURANT MEALS. TOTALLY NON-SMOKING. LUDLOW 8 MILES. S£££, D££.

The Mytton And Mermaid Hotel

Atcham, Shrewsbury, Shropshire SY5 6QG
Tel: 01743 761220 • Fax: 01743 761292

A charming and informal country hotel with the ambience of a traditional wayside inn, this tranquil retreat stands on the banks of the River Severn where the swans glide gracefully through the old arches of Atcham Bridge. It has a relaxed and informal atmosphere aided by comfortable sofas and a log fire. Wines by the glass and locally brewed ale may be enjoyed in company with tasty and imaginative food. Gourmet dining of high order is the reward of a visit to the restaurant where antique oak tables, candles and freshly cut flowers enhance the outstanding cuisine. The Riverside Room is a quiet retreat where one may read, write and enjoy afternoon tea, and the accommodation is in the de luxe category, rooms in the main house and converted stables annexe all having superb appointments.

www.myttonandmermaid.co.uk • e-mail: reception@myttonandmermaid.co.uk

18 BEDROOMS, ALL WITH PRIVATE BATHROOM. ALL BEDROOMS NON-SMOKING. FREE HOUSE WITH REAL ALE. CHILDREN AND PETS WELCOME. BAR AND RESTAURANT MEALS. DESIGNATED COVERED SMOKING AREA. SHREWSBURY 4 MILES. S££££, D£££.

TRAVELLERS REST INN (on facing page)

12 BEDROOM, ALL WITH PRIVATE BATHROOM. FREE HOUSE WITH REAL ALE. PETS WELCOME. BAR MEALS. CRAVEN ARMS 3 MILES. S££, D£.

The Travellers Rest Inn

Upper Affcot, Church Stretton SY6 6RL
Tel: 01694 781275 • Fax: 01694 781555
e-mail: reception@travellersrestinn.co.uk
www.travellersrestinn.co.uk

Situated between Church Stretton and Craven Arms, and surrounded by The South Shropshire Hills. We, Fraser and Mauresia Allison, the owners assure you a warm welcome, good food, good beers, good accommodation, and good old fashioned service.

For those wishing to stay overnight with us at The Travellers Rest we have 12 very nice en suite guest bedrooms: six of these being on the ground floor with easy access, and two of these are suitable for accompanied wheel chair users. The bedrooms are away from the main area of the Inn and have their own entrance to the car park and garden, ideal if you have brought your pet with you and a midnight walk is needed.

Our well stocked Bar can satisfy most thirsts; cask ales, lagers, stouts, spirits, wines and minerals, throughout the day and the Kitchen takes care of your hunger; be it for a snack or a full satisfying meal, vegetarians no problem, food being served until 9pm in the evening.

Staffordshire

Warwickshire

The Coleshill Hotel

152-156 High Street, Coleshill, Warwickshire B46 3BG

Tel: 01675 465 527 • Fax: 01675 464 013 • www.coleshillhotel.com

The Coleshill is a popular haunt, with a heated outdoor terrace and delightfully named fireside 'Nook'. Birmingham NEC is just three miles away, and the city centre is convenient for a burst of retail therapy. Accommodation is spread over two buildings, with a Georgian annexe across the road. Each room is en suite, and rates include a full English breakfast.

The Clarendon House

High Street, Kenilworth, Warwickshire CV8 1LZ

Tel: 01926 857 668 • Fax: 01926 850 669 • www.clarendonhouse-hotel.com

With Warwick Castle and Shakespeare's Stratford nearby, The Clarendon is an ideal point from which to enjoy great family days out. Outdoor types will marvel at the choice of sporting activities in the area. Rooms are en suite, with direct-dial telephone and other standard facilities; rates include full English breakfast.

THE MILLERS HOTEL

Twycross Road, Sibson, Nuneaton, Warwickshire CV13 6LB

Tel: 01827 880 223 • Fax: 01827 880 990 • www.millershotel-sibson.com

Sibson's former village bakery is now a superb conference and training centre and is perfect for weddings and birthday celebrations. Accommodation is en suite with all modern facilities. The Bar/Restaurant serves modern and traditional snacks and meals, real ale and carefully selected wines. Easy access to East Midlands Airport and Birmingham NEC.

Pet-Friendly
Pubs, Inns & Hotels

on pages 174-182

Please note that these establishments may not feature in the main section of this book

Worcestershire

The Anchor Inn
Main Road, Wyre Piddle, Pershore, Worcestershire WR10 2JB
Tel: 01386 556059
Formerly boatmen's cottages, the Anchor Inn has gardens overlooking the beautiful South Worcestershire countryside and a terraced area by the waterside. Draught beers, real ales and wines are available, and the menu features dishes prepared from locally sourced ingredients.

Perdiswell House
Droitwich Road, Worcester, Worcestershire WR3 7JU • Tel: 01905 451311
Popular pub and diner situated on the outskirts of Worcester, with lots of delightful features and facilities to make your visit as relaxing and enjoyable as possible. A children's play area called Fuzzy Ed's Fun House will keep the kids entertained while mum and dad relax.

The Talbot
8-10 Barbourne Road, Worcester, Worcestershire WR1 1HT • Tel: 01905 723744
The Talbot is a candidate for the best pub in town, with a whole host of facilities and weekly entertainment including live music, a pool table, dart board and a beer garden – perfect for alfresco dining in summer months. Dishes on the menu are of a high standard and are prepared from the freshest ingredients.

THE MARWOOD
The Tything, Worcester, Worcestershire WR1 1JL
Tel: 01905 330 460 • www.themarwood.co.uk
Stunning Georgian establishment located in the tranquil Worcestershire countryside, with all traditional features including open log fires, a cosy restaurant and a lavish Champagne Terrace. This pub has character and stands out because of this, offering a good selection of beers, real ales and European lagers.

East Yorkshire

THE WOLDS INN

**Driffield Road, Huggate,
East Yorkshire YO42 IYH
Tel: 01377 288217**

huggate@woldsinn.freeserve.co.uk

A peaceful country inn in farming country high in the Wolds, the hostelry exudes an atmosphere well in keeping with its 16th century origins. Panelling, brassware and crackling fires all contribute to a mood of contentment, well supported in practical terms by splendid food served either in the convivial bar, where meals are served daily at lunchtimes and in the evenings, or in the award-winning restaurant where choice may be made from a mouth-watering à la carte menu. Sunday roasts are also very popular.

Huggate lies on the Wolds Way and the inn is justly popular with walkers, whilst historic York and Beverley and their racecourses and the resorts of Bridlington, Hornsea and Scarborough are within easy reach.

First-rate overnight accommodation is available, all rooms having en suite facilities, central heating, colour television and tea and coffee tray.

3 BEDROOMS, ALL WITH PRIVATE BATHROOM. ALL BEDROOMS NON-SMOKING. FREE HOUSE WITH REAL ALE. CHILDREN WELCOME. BAR MEALS, A LA CARTE MENU IN EVENINGS. POCKLINGTON 6 MILES. S££, D£.

RATES
S – SINGLE ROOM rate   D – Sharing DOUBLE/TWIN ROOM

S£ D£ =Under £35   S££ D££ =£36-£45   S£££ D£££ =£46-£55   S££££ D££££ =Over £55

This is meant as an indication only and does not show prices for Special Breaks, Weekends, etc. Guests are therefore advised to verify all prices on enquiring or booking.

North Yorkshire

The Fox & Hounds Inn

Former 16th century coaching inn, now a high quality residential Country Inn & Restaurant set amidst the beautiful North York Moors. Freshly prepared dishes, using finest local produce, are served every lunchtime and evening, with selected quality wines and a choice of cask ales.
Excellent en suite acccommodation is available.
Open all year. Winter Breaks available November to March.

For bookings please Tel: 01287 660218
Ainthorpe, Danby, Yorkshire YO21 2LD
e-mail: info@foxandhounds-ainthorpe.com
www.foxandhounds-ainthorpe.com

7 BEDROOMS, ALL WITH PRIVATE BATHROOM. ALL BEDROOMS NON-SMOKING. FREE HOUSE WITH REAL ALE. CHILDREN AND PETS WELCOME. BAR AND RESTAURANT MEALS. WHITBY 12 MILES. S£££, D££.

Pet-Friendly
Pubs, Inns & Hotels
on pages 174-182
Please note that these establishments may not feature in the main section of this book

The Cross Keys

Middlesbrough Road, Upsall, Guisborough, North Yorkshire TS14 6RW
Tel: 01287 610035

The Cross Keys is the meeting point for the local branch of CAMRA, and offers all the traditional attractions of the classic English pub, such as low oak beams, wood-panelled recesses and a beer garden where guests have the option of dining alfresco. 20 bedrooms with all modern facilities provide comfortable accommodation.

The Claro Beagle

Ripon Road, Harrogate, North Yorkshire HG1 2JJ • Tel: 01423 569974

A modern-style community pub, with a contemporary bright, fresh look. There is a sports area with pool tables, a dart board and a plasma screen showing live sporting fixtures. Free wifi facility throughout.

THE TRAVELLER'S REST

Crimple Lane, Crimple, Harrogate, North Yorkshire HG3 1DF
Tel: 01423 883960

An old fashioned, traditional public house near Harrogate town centre, with low oak beams, a delightful stone-floored section and a charming conservatory leading to the garden area, where alfresco diners can enjoy views of sheep, ducks and swans. Real ales and draught beers are served chilled during summer months.

The Squinting Cat

Lund House Green, Pannal Ash, Harrogate, North Yorkshire HG3 1QF
Tel: 01423 565650

The Squinting Cat is a Two For One public house set in rural surroundings just south of the town centre. Families love to come here for mouth-watering dishes at affordable prices, and facilities include a children's 'Wacky Warehouse' play area and a large beer garden.

The *New Inn*
BURNT YATES

Situated on the doorstep to the Yorkshire Dales, in the village of Burnt Yates, this beautifully maintained, traditional inn first opened its doors as a hostelry in 1810; today it combines the perfect ingredients for an enjoyable lunch or evening out: a genuine warm welcome, expertly kept real ales, fine wines and delicious food, all home-cooked using high quality local produce.
★★★★ **for Accommodation, Food and Service**

Comfortable en suite bedrooms make an ideal base for a truly memorable stay. The beautiful spa town of Harrogate is only a ten minute drive away and you are within easy reach of some of the finest countryside in Britain.

Burnt Yates, Harrogate, North Yorkshire HG3 3EG
Tel: 01423 771070 • Fax: 01423 772360

e-mail: newinnharrogate@btconnect.com • www.thenewinnburntyates.co.uk

8 BEDROOMS, ALL WITH PRIVATE BATHROOM. REAL ALE. CHILDREN AND PETS WELCOME.
RESTAURANT MEALS. RIPLEY 2 MILES. S£££££, D££-££££.

THE
FORRESTERS ARMS
HOTEL

www.forrestersarms.fsnet.co.uk

Dating from the 12th century, this is one
of England's oldest inns.
The Henry Dee Bar still retains evidence
of the days when it was the stable and
the cosy lower bar has an unusual rounded
stone chimney breast where log fires
exude cheer in chilly weather.
Both bars are furnished with the work of Robert Thompson (the 'Mouseman') who
carved a tiny mouse on every piece of furniture produced. Real ale is available in
convivial surroundings and ample and well-presented Yorkshire fare will
more than satisfy the healthiest appetite.
This is the heart of James Herriot Country, within the North York
Moors National Park, and the hotel is well recommended as a touring
base, having outstanding accommodation.

English Tourism Council
GUEST ACCOMMODATION

AA
★★

The Forresters Arms, Kilburn, North Yorkshire YO61 4AH
Tel: 01347 868386 • e-mail: fiona@forrestersarms.com • www.forrestersarms.com

10 BEDROOMS, ALL WITH PRIVATE BATHROOM. FREE HOUSE WITH REAL ALE. CHILDREN AND PETS WELCOME.
BAR AND RESTAURANT MEALS. NON-SMOKING AREAS. THIRSK 6 MILES. S£££, D£.

𝕲olden 𝕷ion HOTEL
Market Place, Leyburn, North Yorkshire DL8 5AS

Tel: 01969 622161
Fax: 01969 623836
info@goldenlionleyburn.co.uk

At the gateway to Wensleydale, this splendid hotel dates from
1765, although it has been tastefully modernised. Light meals
and afternoon teas are served in the bars, and the restaurant with
its picture windows and colourful murals is a popular venue.
Excellent accommodation is available in rooms with bathrooms
en suite, television, telephone, radio and tea and coffee-
makers. A lift operates to all floors. Within easy walking
distance is the little town of Middleham on the River Ure
which is well known as a racehorse training centre.

English Tourism Council
★
HOTEL

14 BEDROOMS, ALL WITH PRIVATE BATHROOM. FREE HOUSE WITH REAL ALE. CHILDREN AND PETS WELCOME.
BAR AND RESTAURANT MEALS. NON-SMOKING AREAS. RICHMOND 8 MILES. S££, D££.

The Crown Inn

High Street, Knaresborough, North Yorkshire HG5 0HB • Tel: 01423 862122

A friendly venue showing live sporting fixtures and hosting regular pool tournaments, the Crown is perfect for a relaxed lunchtime outing or an early evening meal with family or friends. Live music and regular entertainment are popular features.

The Coulby Farm

Coulby Newham, Middlesbrough, North Yorkshire TS8 9DZ
Tel: 01642 594140 • Fax: 01642 590404

The Coulby is a family pub, with good children's facilities and a Two For One food menu to suit all ages. The decor is a pleasant mix of creams and browns with leather sofas, and facilities include a large Fun House with ball pits, slides, and climbing frames.

The Rudd's Arms

Marton, Middlesbrough, North Yorkshire TS7 8BG • Tel: 01642 315262

After a substantial makeover, the Rudd's Arms features chic furnishings and fittings and a new open-plan layout. The pub is well known for its good quality food, including tapas and breakfast menus and for serving an extensive range of drinks. There are regular quiz nights, plus free wifi and a decked seating area.

The Norman Conquest

Flatts Lane, Middlesbrough, North Yorkshire TS6 0NP • Tel: 01642 454000

A family pub where food is served throughout the day from an inventive menu; customers can dine anywhere in the open plan layout or in the beer garden. Activities include a weekly quiz, karaoke and live entertainment. Children welcome.

THE SOUTHERN CROSS

Dixons Bank, Middlesbrough, North Yorkshire TS7 8NX • Tel: 01642 317539

A large pub situated on a main road in the suburbs of Middlesbrough. Downstairs is a sports bar with four plasma screens, so there's no chance of missing that all important football match. The Two for One Menu is very popular amongst the locals at lunchtimes, and there are regular quizzes and live music.

The Three Jolly Sailors

Burniston, Scarborough, North Yorkshire YO13 0HJ • Tel: 01723 871628

Situated in the quaint village of Burniston just north of Scarborough is this Grade II Listed pub, an ideal stopoff point for ramblers on the Smugglers Walk between Scarborough and Whitby. All dishes are freshly prepared from locally sourced ingredients whenever possible.

The Scarborough

Market Lane, Eastfield, Scarborough, North Yorkshire YO11 3YN
Tel: 01723 582444 • Fax: 01723 582443

A Hungry Horse pub serving food and drink over four floors, with a children's play area on the top floor – a safe and secure place to keep youngsters entertained while parents relax. There is a beer garden, and regular events include pool competitions, karaoke and DJ/fun nights.

The Griffin

42 Micklegate, Selby, North Yorkshire YO8 0EQ
Tel: 01757 703227 • Fax: 01757 704574

A popular spot on the market square in Selby, recently refurbished to create an uplifting atmosphere, with contemporary lighter shades and stylish furnishings. Regular activities include three pool tables, a weekly quiz, karaoke and a live DJ at weekends.

The Londesborough Hotel

Market Place, Selby, North Yorkshire YO8 4NS
Tel: 01757 707355 • Fax: 01757 701607

Brimming with tradition, this friendly bar stocks a good selection of beers, ales and wines, and the kitchen brigade prepares quality meals to suit all tastes. Accommodation is in 23 Laura Ashley-style luxury bedrooms, almost all en suite.

Ye Olde Three Tuns

11 Finkle Street, Thirsk, North Yorkshire YO7 1DA • Tel: 01845 523291

As its name suggests, The Tuns is the oldest pub in this lively market town. Tradition is paramount, and the pub's original features include low oak beams and open log fires. Live sporting fixtures are shown regularly on the large-screen TV, making it popular with supporters celebrating the victory of their favourite rugby and football teams.

The Windmill

16 - 20 Blossom Street, York, North Yorkshire YO24 1AJ • Tel: 01904 624834

This is a popular and contemporary venue situated in York centre. The menu offers an ample choice of delicious dishes and the bar is stocked with a wide range of drinks. Comfortable accommodation and good service make this an even more attractive prospect.

THE KNAVESMIRE

Albemarke Road, York, North Yorkshire YO23 1ER • Tel: 01904 655927

Located 200 yards from York racecourses, this attractive sports and entertainment bar is well equipped to satisfy all requirements, with four pool tables, a video jukebox, and a bar stocked with a wide range of beers, lagers, ales and wines.

Lendal Cellars

26 Lendal, York, North Yorkshire YO1 8AA • Tel: 01904 623121

Traditional cellar bar situated in the picturesque city of York, with food available from an exciting menu including burgers and other pub food favourites. The bar is well stocked, with guest real ales, lagers, beers and wines. Features include an open-mic night, live bands and an outdoor pool table. Children welcome when dining.

South Yorkshire

Northumberland

Family-Friendly
Pubs, Inns & Hotels
See the Supplement on pages 183-186 for establishments which really welcome children

RATES

Normal Bed & Breakfast rate per person **(single room)**		Normal Bed & Breakfast rate per person **(sharing double/twin room)**	
PRICE RANGE	CATEGORY	PRICE RANGE	CATEGORY
Under £35	S£	Under £35	D£
£36-£45	S££	£36-£45	D££
£46-£55	S£££	£46-£55	D£££
Over £55	S££££	Over £55	D££££

This is meant as an indication only and does not show prices for Special Breaks, Weekends, etc. Guests are therefore advised to verify all prices on enquiring or booking.

THE OLDE SHIP HOTEL

Main Street,
Seahouses,
Northumberland
NE68 7RD
Tel: 01665 720200
Fax: 01665 720283

A former farmhouse dating from 1745, the inn stands overlooking the harbour in the village of Seahouses.

The Olde Ship, first licensed in 1812, has been in the same family for over 90 years and is now a fully residential hotel. All guest rooms, including three with four-poster beds, and executive suites with lounges and sea views, are en suite, with television, refreshment facilities and direct-dial telephone. The bars and corridors bulge at the seams with nautical memorabilia. Good home cooking features locally caught seafood, along with soups, puddings and casseroles

www.seahouses.co.uk • e-mail: theoldeship@seahouses.co.uk

18 BEDROOMS, ALL WITH PRIVATE BATHROOM. ALL BEDROOMS NON-SMOKING. FREE HOUSE WITH REAL ALE.
CHILDREN OVER 10 YEARS WELCOME IF STAYING IN HOTEL. BAR AND RESTAURANT MEALS.
BAMBURGH 3 MILES. S££, D££££.

Tyne & Wear

The Gold Medal

Chowdene Bank, Gateshead, Tyne and Wear NE9 6JP • Tel: 0191 4821549

Family pub situated in Gateshead, where drinks and food are served with a smile and both are reasonably priced and generous in quantity. There is regular entertainment, perhaps a quiz, live music, or even live sporting fixtures shown on the big screen.

The Guide Post

Makepeace Terrace, Springwell, Gateshead, Tyne & Wear NE9 7RR
Tel: 0191 4160298 • Fax: 0191 4179841

Situated between Gateshead and Washington, this popular spot attracts a friendly crowd made up of students, regulars and passers by. The food menu is popular, particularly the Sunday Roasts. Attractions include a pool table, dart board, and a big screen TV, plus regular quizzes and live music.

The Beaconsfield

Beaconsfield Road, Low Fell, Gateshead, Tyne and Wear NE9 5EU • Tel: 0191 4820125

Shades of cream, red ochre and sage green, plus suede seats and oak flooring, enhance the elegant decor of this modern venue in Gateshead. Hot and cold snacks are served throughout the day, every day, and live sporting fixtures are shown on large plasma screens.

Family-Friendly
Pubs, Inns & Hotels
See the Supplement on pages 183-186 for establishments
which really welcome children

THE LONSDALE

West Jesmond, Newcastle-upon-Tyne, Tyne & Wear NE2 3HQ • Tel: 0191 2810039
Students love this pub venue situated in a popular area just outside West Jesmond.
Customers enjoy the live sporting fixtures shown on the big screens, plasma screen or
one of the other TVs. Attractions include two pool tables, quiz nights and live bands.

The Corner House

Heaton, Newcastle-upon-Tyne, Tyne & Wear NE6 5RP • Tel: 0191 2659602
Open-plan corner pub with a distinctive long bar, ideal for an after-work drink or meal.
The staff are welcoming and add to the relaxed atmosphere. Facilities include a pool
table, dart board, quizzes and big screen TVs. Accommodation is in 10 bedrooms
(double, twin and family), all with modern facilities.

The Newton Park

Longbenton, Newcastle-upon-Tyne, Tyne & Wear NE7 7EB
Tel: 0191 266 2010 • www.newtonparkheaton.co.uk
Situated next to the Ministry in Benton Park, this U-shaped open-plan bar
boasts comfortable sofas and an imaginative food menu. Attractions include
a games room, real ale bar, function room and dining area.

The Eye on The Tyne

Broad Chare, Newcastle-upon-Tyne, Tyne & Wear NE1 3DQ • Tel: 0191 2617385
Located in the middle of a prestigious part of the city centre, close to local hotels, and
with the Law Courts nearby, this pub attracts a varied clientele. The in-house coffee
shop serves coffee and freshly prepared food from 11am.

The Crows Nest

Percy Street, Newcastle-upon-Tyne, Tyne & Wear NE1 7RY • Tel: 0191 2612607
Formerly Bar Oz, the theme is fun, with fantastic food! Convenient for the two
universities of Newcastle and Northumbria, the pub is very popular with students.
It offers a good choice of draught beers and real ales, with a lively atmosphere
during big matches shown on TV.

The Bourgognes

78 Newgate Street, Newcastle upon Tyne, Tyne & Wear NE1 5RQ • Tel: 0191 2326212
Located next to Eldon Square shopping centre and just a short distance from St James'
football ground. With leather couches, wooden floors and carpeted recesses, this
friendly pub is popular with students who appreciate the reasonably priced fare.

The Bridge

Castle Square, Newcastle upon Tyne, Tyne & Wear NE1 1RQ • Tel: 0191 2326400
This pub couldn't be in a better location, facing the Castle Keep and overlooking the Tyne. The interior is of a high standard, having undergone a substantial refurbishment. Attractions include six cask beers, live music and a mouth-watering food menu.

The Gunner

Trevor Place, North Shields, Tyne & Wear NE30 2DH • Tel: 0191 2574682
Geordie pub built in the 1960s, located in a residential area of North Shields. On sporting occasions, the L-shaped venue becomes packed with supporters glued to the two big screens. Food is served all day every day, and amenities include a pool table, dart board, and delightful beer garden.

The Bamburgh

175 Bamburgh Avenue, South Shields, Tyne & Wear NE34 6SS • Tel: 0191 4541899
Those familiar with South Shields will know that its seafront is most attractive, and The Bamburgh offers unparalleled views of the coast and piers. Nicely decorated, with laminate flooring and leather sofas, this is an ideal spot for meeting friends. Facilities include pool tables and a dart board.

The Monkseaton Arms

Monkseaton, Whitley Bay, Tyne & Wear NE25 8DP • Tel: 0191 2513928
Named after monks who ran the brewery when this building was a monastery, today retro touches and comfy leather seating contribute to the relaxed atmosphere of this friendly establishment. Coffee is served here throughout the day and there is free wifi access.

RATES

Normal Bed & Breakfast rate per person (single room)		Normal Bed & Breakfast rate per person (sharing double/twin room)	
PRICE RANGE	CATEGORY	PRICE RANGE	CATEGORY
Under £35	S£	Under £35	D£
£36-£45	S££	£36-£45	D££
£46-£55	S£££	£46-£55	D£££
Over £55	S££££	Over £55	D££££

This is meant as an indication only and does not show prices for Special Breaks, Weekends, etc. Guests are therefore advised to verify all prices on enquiring or booking.

Cheshire

The Pheasant Inn

Tucked in a peaceful corner of rural Cheshire, the 300-year-old Pheasant Inn at Higher Burwardsley stands atop the Peckforton Hills, with the most magnificent panoramic views of the Cheshire plains. Whether you come to drink, dine or unwind for a few days in one of our 12 en suite bedrooms, this atmospheric location will quickly have you under its spell. Freshly cooked wholesome food using local produce is on the menu, rewarded for its quality with an AA Rosette, and listing in the Michelin Good Pub Guide and Egon Ronay Guide. Delightful old sandstone buildings, open log fires, and the friendly, cosy atmosphere all add to the magic!

The Pheasant Inn
Higher Burwardsley, Tattenhall
Cheshire CH3 9PF
Tel: 01829 770434 • Fax: 01829 771097
e-mail: info@thepheasantinn.co.uk • www.thepheasantinn.co.uk

12 BEDROOMS, ALL WITH PRIVATE BATHROOM. FREE HOUSE WITH REAL ALE. CHILDREN AND PETS WELCOME. BAR AND RESTAURANT MEALS. NON-SMOKING AREAS. CHESTER 9 MILES. S£££, D££.

Pet-Friendly
Pubs, Inns & Hotels
on pages 174-182
Please note that these establishments may not feature in the main section of this book

The Plough
AT EATON

**Macclesfield Road, Eaton,
Near Congleton, Cheshire CW12 2NH
Tel: 01260 280207 • Fax: 01260 298458**

Traditional oak beams and blazing log fires in winter reflect the warm and friendly atmosphere of this half-timbered former coaching inn which dates from the 17th century.

The heart of the 'Plough' is the kitchen where food skilfully prepared is calculated to satisfy the most discerning palate. Luncheons and dinners are served seven days a week with traditional roasts on Sundays.

In peaceful, rolling countryside near the Cheshire/Staffordshire border, this is a tranquil place in which to stay and the hostelry has elegantly colour-co-ordinated guest rooms, all with spacious bathrooms, LCD colour television, direct-dial telephone and tea and coffee-making facilities amongst their impressive appointments. Wireless internet access available.

**e-mail: theploughinn@hotmail.co.uk
www.theploughinnateaton.co.uk**

The De Trafford

Congleton Road, Alderley Edge, Cheshire SK9 7AA
Tel: 01625 583881 • Fax: 01625 586625

Cobblestone surroundings lead prospective visitors to this elegant inn located in Alderley Edge. Tradition is paramount, with open fires, candlelit tables and cosy nooks for private dining. Accommodation is next door – all bedrooms are en suite, with colour TV and tea/coffee making facilities.

The Shrewsbury Arms

Warrington Road, Mickle Trafford, Chester, Cheshire CH2 4EB • Tel: 01244 300309

The Shrewsbury Arms has everything one could want in a country pub – low oak beams, slate flooring and an impressive stock of cask ales, fine wines and beers. The pub's menu features traditional favourites prepared from fresh fish and locally sourced meat, and a Sunday Roast.

The Oaklands

93 Hoole Road, Chester, Cheshire CH2 3NB • Tel: 01244 345528

A peaceful spot set in an idyllic part of Chester, serving real ales, fine wines and hearty pub meals. There is regular entertainment, and large TV screens mean you can count on the Oaklands for those all-important football matches!

Bromfield Arms

43 Faulkener Street, Chester, Cheshire CH2 3BD • Tel: 01244 345037

Located close to the zoo in Chester is this Cask Marque accredited pub with a pool room and snug. Customers need no encouragement to sample the real ales and delicious meals on offer. There is a weekly quiz, and live sporting fixtures are shown on a large screen TV.

THE WHITE LION

Manley Road, Alvanley, Frodsham, Cheshire WA6 9DD • Tel: 01928 722949

Alvanley is an idyllic location with breathtaking views all around. The White Lion upholds all the traditional pub values, with wooden beams, good food and the warmth of two real fires in winter. There is a good choice of quality wines, real ales and draught beers.

THE PLOUGH AT EATON (on facing page)

17 BEDROOMS, ALL WITH PRIVATE BATHROOM. ALL BEDROOMS NON-SMOKING. FREE HOUSE WITH REAL ALE. CHILDREN WELCOME. BAR AND RESTAURANT MEALS. CONGLETON 2 MILES. S££££, D££££.

The Three Greyhounds

Holmes Chapel Road, Allostock, Knutsford, Cheshire WA16 9JY • Tel: 01565 722234

A traditional pub with all the trimmings - a taproom, snug and open fireplaces.
Meals are prepared from fresh local ingredients and the variety of dishes is spectacular;
beers, ales and wines are carefully selected and plentiful.
Dogs are welcome at this establishment.

The Egerton Arms

Knutsford Road, Chelford, Macclesfield, Cheshire SK11 9BB
Tel: 01625 861366 • www.chelfordegertonarms.co.uk

Family-run pub situated in Cheshire countryside, where customers can expect the very
best real ales and local sourced cuisine. The decor is in keeping with traditional pub
values, with open fireplaces, antiques, low wooden beams and brass pumps at the bar.
Facilities include a pool table and dart board.

The Rose & Crown

Allgreave, Macclesfield, Cheshire SK11 0BJ • Tel: 01260 227232

Located in a breathtaking Peak District setting overlooking the Dane Valley, this
establishment is very popular with dog walkers and tourists. For those who find it
difficult to leave this delightful pub, there is the option of bed and breakfast – each
bedroom is en suite, with colour TV and tea/coffee making facilities.

The Legh Arms

London Road, Adlington, Macclesfield, Cheshire SK10 4NA • Tel: 01625 829211

This is the ideal place to meet friends for a coffee, or simply relax over a pint of your
favourite ale. The carvery serves dishes prepared from British produce, with a choice of
four different roasts. Customers are guaranteed good service and a warm welcome!

THE BUTLEY ASH

Butley, Prestbury, Macclesfield, Cheshire SK10 4EA • Tel: 01625 829207

The only pub in the tiny hamlet of Butley near Macclesfield, retaining traditional
features such as wooden beams and antique furniture. The menu offers a wide choice,
including fish dishes, and the bar has a good stock of wines, beers and real ale.

The Forester's Arms

92-94 High Street, Tarporley, Cheshire CW6 0AX
Tel: 01829 733151• www.theforesters.co.uk • foresters-arms@btconnect.com

A picture-perfect inn convenient for local attractions and within easy reach of golf
courses, motor racing circuits, ancient castles, racing stables and Beeston market.
Accommodation is in single, twin and double bedrooms, all en suite; rates include full
English breakfast. The nearest main railway stations are Chester and Crewe.

Cumbria

THE EASTERN FELLS, Lake District...*where dogs stay for **free**!*

the mardale inn @ st. patrick's well
Bampton, Cumbria, CA10 2RQ

Early 18th century Lake District inn. Fresh local food served all day including £5 two-course Farmer's Meal on weekday lunch times (please ring for a table). Hand pulled Cumbrian real ales plus regular guest ale and great wines. Extensive bottled beer list. Fine accommodation. Fantastic walking around nearby Haweswater. Real fires and a warm welcome. Featured in Daily Telegraph '50 Best Pubs' - May '08.

www.mardaleinn.co.uk
info@mardaleinn.co.uk

ETC
★★★★

tel: 01931 713244

Children and dogs welcome *(please note that children must be kept on a short leash at all times!)*

the greyhound @ shap   **Main St, Shap, CA10 2PW**

The Greyhound @ Shap is a perfect motorway stop-off on the edge of the Lake District. M6 J39 only 5 minutes. Coaching Inn dating from the 15th century. Hand pulled real ales plus regular guest ales. Extensive wine list (also available by the glass). Traditional local food served daily. Great walks from the door onto the Eastern fells. 10 bedrooms with en-suite facilities. Families and walkers welcome. Fantastic Sunday lunch!

tel: 01931 716474

www.greyhoundshap.co.uk
info@greyhoundshap.co.uk

Always open—fresh local produce—open fires—fine cask beers—warm beds

---

MARDALE INN: 4 BEDROOMS, ALL WITH PRIVATE BATHROOM. ALL BEDROOMS NON-SMOKING. FREE HOUSE WITH REAL ALE. CHILDREN AND PETS WELCOME. BAR MEALS, RESTAURANT EVENINGS ONLY. SHAP 3 MILES. S££, D££.

GREYHOUND: 10 BEDROOMS, ALL WITH PRIVATE BATHROOM. ALL BEDROOMS NON-SMOKING. ENTERPRISE INNS HOUSE WITH REAL ALE. CHILDREN AND PETS WELCOME. BAR AND RESTAURANT MEALS. SHAP 3 MILES. S££, D££.

Please mention **FHG's Pubs & Inns of Britain**
when making enquiries about accommodation featured in these pages

The Turk's Head

Market Square, Alston, Cumbria CA9 3HS • Tel: 01434 381148

For those in search of an olde world bar with the very best in draught beers and real ales – this is the place. Food is served in the lounge bar at the rear of the pub.

The Sportsman Inn

Compston Road, Ambleside, Cumbria LA22 9DR • Tel: 01539 432535

Set in the lovely village of Ambleside is this welcoming pub and lounge bar. Food is served throughout the day from an extensive menu of pub food favourites. There is an upstairs bar and a basement bar, where discos are regularly held.

SAWREY HOTEL

Far Sawrey, Near Ambleside, Cumbria LA22 0LQ

This fully licensed 18th century free house stands within easy reach of all parts of Lakeland, just one mile from Windermere car ferry and 2½ miles from Hawkshead. It is an ideal centre for touring, walking, pony trekking and sailing, and all the other activities that this beautiful area is renowned for.

There are 18 bedrooms, all with colour TV, tea/coffee facilities, telephone and private bathrooms. Excellent cuisine is available in the restaurant, and the Claife Crier Bar serves an extensive range of hot and cold snacks. Under the personal management of the proprietors.

Tel: 015394 43425 • Fax: 015394 48341 • ETC ★★

The Sun Inn

www.dentbrewery.co.uk

Main Street, Dent, Sedbergh, Cumbria LA10 5QL
Tel: 01539 625208 • e-mail: thesun@dentbrewery.co.uk

Dent, with its quaint narrow cobbled street lined with stone cottages, some dating from the 15th and 16th centuries, is within the Yorkshire Dales National Park and, completely unspoiled, is a most relaxing holiday venue. So, too, is the Sun's bar, a convivial retreat that will soon cast its spell on all who enter, a happy mood influenced not only by its coin-studded beams, open coal fire and fascinating collection of local photographs, but also by its traditional ales and tempting variety of straightforward meals.

A homely place in which to stay, this friendly hostelry has comfortable rooms with washbasin, colour television and tea and coffee-making facilities.

4 BEDROOMS. DENT BREWERY HOUSE WITH REAL ALE. CHILDREN AND PETS WELCOME. BAR MEALS. NON-SMOKING AREAS. SEDBERGH 4 MILES. S£, D£.

The Shepherds Arms Hotel

A gem of a country house hotel and inn, offering first-rate en suite accommodation, an extensive bar menu of home-cooked dishes, and a fine selection of real ales. Ennerdale Bridge is situated on one of the most beautiful stretches of Wainwright's Coast to Coast Walk and very popular with walkers.

The hotel has two twin and two double en suite bedrooms, and one twin/one small double room with private bath and shower. All are non-smoking and have telephone, digital TV, radio alarm, and tea/coffee making facilities. Breakfast is served in the Georgian panelled dining room. Complement your meal with a selection of fine wines and relax afterwards in the comfortable lounge with its open log fire.

The Shepherds Arms bar is open to the public and is included in *The Good Pub Guide* and CAMRA *Good Beer Guide*. Specialities are real ales and home-cooked locally sourced produce from the extensive bar menu. Packed lunches and bikes for hire.

Ennerdale Bridge, Lake District National Park CA23 3AR
Tel: 01946 861249
e-mail: shepherdsarms@btconnect.com
www.shepherdsarmshotel.co.uk

6 BEDROOMS, ALL WITH PRIVATE BATHROOM. ALL BEDROOMS NON-SMOKING. FREE HOUSE WITH REAL ALE. CHILDREN AND PETS WELCOME. BAR MEALS. WHITEHAVEN 8 MILES. S£££, D£££.

Family-Friendly
Pubs, Inns & Hotels

See the Supplement on pages 183-186 for establishments which really welcome children

Horse and Farrier Inn
Threlkeld, Keswick CA12 4SQ

Situated beneath Blencathra, in an ideal location for walking or touring the Lake District. All 15 bedrooms en suite, with TV, tea/coffee making and hairdryer. Award-winning food and restaurant. Open all year. Pets welcome.
Tel: **017687 79688** • Fax: **017687 79823**
info@horseandfarrier.com
www.horseandfarrier.com

9 BEDROOMS, ALL WITH PRIVATE BATHROOM. FREE HOUSE WITH REAL ALE. CHILDREN WELCOME.
BAR AND RESTAURANT MEALS. KESWICK 4 MILES.

Coledale INN
Braithwaite,
Near Keswick CA12 5TN
Tel: 017687 78272
Fax: 017687 78416

A friendly, family-run Victorian Inn in a peaceful hillside position above Braithwaite, and ideally situated for touring and walking, with paths to the mountains immediately outside our gardens. All bedrooms are warm and spacious, with en suite shower room and colour television. Children are welcome, as are pets. Home-cooked meals are served every lunchtime and evening, with a fine selection of inexpensive wines, beers and Jennings, Yates and Theakstons real cask ale. Open all year except midweek lunches in winter. Tariff and menu sent on request.

www.coledale-inn.co.uk
info@coledale-inn.co.uk

20 BEDROOMS, ALL WITH PRIVATE BATHROOM. FREE HOUSE WITH REAL ALE. CHILDREN AND PETS WELCOME.
BAR AND RESTAURANT MEALS. NON-SMOKING AREAS. KESWICK 2 MILES. S£, D£.

Barbon Inn

Barbon,
Near Kirkby Lonsdale
Cumbria LA6 2LJ
Tel & Fax: 015242 76233

If you are torn between the scenic delights of the Lake District and the Yorkshire Dales, then you can have the best of both worlds by making your base this friendly 17th century coaching inn nestling in the pretty village of Barbon.

Individually furnished bedrooms provide cosy accommodation, and for that extra touch of luxury enquire about the elegant mini-suite with its mahogany four-poster bed.

Fresh local produce is featured on the good value menus presented in the bar and restaurant, and the

Sunday roast lunch with all the trimmings attracts patrons from near and far. A wide range of country pursuits can be enjoyed in the immediate area

Bedrooms, dining room and lounge non-smoking.

www.barbon-inn.co.uk

10 BEDROOMS, ALL WITH PRIVATE BATHROOM. ALL BEDROOMS NON-SMOKING. FREE HOUSE WITH REAL ALE. CHILDREN AND PETS WELCOME. BAR AND RESTAURANT MEALS. KIRKBY LONSDALE 3 MILES. S£££, D££££.

Cumbria - The Lake District is often described as the most beautiful corner of England, and it's easy to see why 15 million visitors head here every year. It is a place of unrivalled beauty, with crystal clear lakes, bracken-covered mountains, peaceful forests, quiet country roads and miles of stunning coastline.

At the heart of Cumbria is the Lake District National Park. Each of the lakes that make up the area has its own charm and personality: Windermere, England's longest lake, is surrounded by rolling hills; Derwentwater and Ullswater are circled by craggy fells; England's deepest lake, Wastwater, is dominated by high mountains including the country's highest, Scafell Pike. For those who want to tackle the great outdoors, Cumbria offers everything from rock climbing to fell walking and from canoeing to horse riding – all among stunning scenery.

Cumbria has many delightful market towns, historic houses and beautiful gardens such as Holker Hall with its 25 acres of award-winning grounds. There are many opportunities to sample local produce, such as Cumbrian fell-bred lamb, Cumberland Sausage, and trout and salmon plucked fresh from nearby lakes and rivers.

Cumbria is a county of contrasts with a rich depth of cultural and historical interest in addition to stunning scenery. Compact and accessible, it can offer something for every taste.

Nestling in the delightful hamlet of Troutbeck, in the heart of the Lake District National Park and with spectacular views of the surrounding fells, our charming family-run Inn has everything you need for a relaxing break, and to sample everything the Lakes have to offer.

We have seven delightful bedrooms, all en suite, and three beautiful self-catering cottages.

Our restaurant is renowned for its excellent home made food which is all sourced locally, and for our fine wines and real ales.

The Troutbeck Inn
Troutbeck, Penrith, Cumbria CAII 0SJ • Tel: 017684 83635
e-mail: info@thetroutbeckinn.co.uk • www.thetroutbeckinn.co.uk

7 BEDROOMS, ALL WITH PRIVATE BATHROOM. FREE HOUSE WITH REAL ALE. ALL BEDROOMS NON-SMOKING. CHILDREN AND PETS WELCOME. BAR AND RESTAURANT MEALS. KESWICK 8 MILES. S£££, D££££.

The Greyhound Hotel

Main Street, Shap, Penrith, Cumbria CA10 3PW

Established in 1680, the Greyhound offers comfortable accommodation in 11 en suite rooms with colour TV and hostess trays. There is an extensive menu of freshly prepared dishes, including vegetarian choices, using locally bred or grown ingredients where possible. You can eat either in the cosy bar with its open fireplace or in the restaurant.

For tourists Shap is ideal, having easy access to all parts of the Lake District and Northern England, including Howgill and the North Pennine fells and valley. Local attractions include:

Historic houses & castles • Ullswater • Haweswater • Shap Abbey
Limestone Pavements • Extensive walking • Historic Penrith & Kendal

Tel: 01931 716474 ~ Fax: 01931 716305
e-mail: postmaster@greyhoundshap.demon.co.uk
www.greyhoundshap.co.uk

Just off the M6 at Junction 39

10 BEDROOMS, ALL WITH PRIVATE BATHROOM. FREE HOUSE WITH REAL ALE. CHILDREN AND PETS WELCOME. BAR AND RESTAURANT MEALS. PENRITH 9 MILES. S££, D£.

THE
STORK
HOTEL

The Stork Hotel
Rowrah Road, Rowrah CA26 3XJ
Tel: 01946 861213
www.storkhotel.co.uk
e-mail: joan@storkhotel.co.uk

◆ Six newly refurbished rooms, all en suite, with power shower, tea/coffee making and hairdryer.

◆ Extensive menu of home-made dishes prepared from fresh local produce.

◆ Local real ales, as well as popular ciders, lagers and beers.

◆ Situated on the edge of the village, with a wonderful view of the surrounding fells.

◆ Ideal for Coast to Coast Cycle Way, and two miles from Ennerdale village, first stop for Coast to Coast walkers.

◆ Free pickup and drop-off service for guests.

THE STORK HOTEL (on facing page)

6 BEDROOMS, ALL WITH PRIVATE BATHROOM. REAL ALE. BAR MEALS. ENNERDALE 2 MILES.

Lancashire

THE FARMERS' ARMS

Way back in the 17th century, weary travellers called this fine old pub the 'Pleasant Retreat' (the inn was renamed in 1902). Very much a Rothwell family concern, this attractive country hostelry retains its old-world charm and continues to provide good wholesome fare accompanied by traditional, hand-pulled cask ales. Here is all the warmth and appeal of a typical English wayside inn.

Quality en suite four-poster, double, twin and single rooms are available, all with showers, colour television and tea and coffee-makers.

Wood Lane, Heskin, Near Chorley, Lancashire PR7 5NP
Tel: 01257 451276 • Fax: 01257 453958 • www.farmersarms.co.uk

★★★
INN

5 BEDROOMS, ALL WITH PRIVATE BATHROOM. ENTERPRISE INNS HOUSE WITH REAL ALE. CHILDREN WELCOME. BAR AND RESTAURANT MEALS. NON-SMOKING AREAS. CHORLEY 4 MILES. S££, D£.

The Waterside Inn

Twist Lane, Leigh, Lancashire WN7 4DB • Tel: 01942 605005

This Lancashire pub situated next to the canal was formerly a warehouse, and is an ideal place to come for a business lunch, or to catch up with friends over dinner or evening drinks. There is a beer garden to the side, and at the rear decking overlooks the canal.

Pet-Friendly
Pubs, Inns & Hotels
on pages 174-182
Please note that these establishments may not feature in the main section of this book

RATES   S – SINGLE ROOM rate   D – Sharing DOUBLE/TWIN ROOM

S£ D£ =Under £35   S££ D££ =£36-£45   S£££ D£££ =£46-£55   S££££ D££££ =Over £55

This is meant as an indication only and does not show prices for Special Breaks, Weekends, etc.
Guests are therefore advised to verify all prices on enquiring or booking.

Greater Manchester

The Stamford Arms

The Firs, Bowdon, Altrincham, Greater Manchester WA14 2TW • Tel: 0161 9281536

A quintessential English pub standing opposite handsome St Mary's Church, with low-beamed ceilings and a spacious function room. With live sporting fixtures shown on big screens and high quality real ales, there's no reason not to drop in and stay for a while!

The Moss Trooper

Timperley, Altrincham, Greater Manchester WA15 6JU • Tel: 0161 9804610

The Moss Trooper is a CAMRA award-winning pub boasting a heated outdoor seating area, and a stylish interior with comfy sofas and inglenook fires. There is a cosy dining area with candlelit tables, plus an extensive range of wines, ales and beers.

The Old Pelican Inn

Manchester Road, West Timperley, Greater Manchester WA14 5NH
Tel: 0161 9627414 • Fax: 0161 9739144

Spacious 100-year-old inn located in West Timperley, popular with football supporters who enjoy watching live sporting fixtures over a pint of their favourite beer or ale. Food from the John Barras menu is available throughout the day.

The Cotton Kier

Watersmeeting Road, Bolton, Greater Manchester BL1 8TS
Tel: 01204 363010 Fax: 01204 559797

Situated on the outskirts of Bolton, this friendly family pub has a contemporary, light interior. The menu offers a wide choice of dishes, and entertainment comes in the form of a weekly quiz.

The Three Pigeons

820 Wigan Road, Bolton, Greater Manchester BL3 4RD • Tel: 01204 61678

This friendly pub features live sporting fixtures shown on big screens, plus a food menu with a wide range of meals. Facilities are excellent here and include a beer garden, a pool table, and quiz and bowling machines.

The Hare & Hounds

Holcombe Brook, Ramsbottom, Bury, Greater Manchester BL0 9RY • Tel: 01706 822107

Set in rambling countryside with open moorland nearby, this friendly pub dates back to the 1600s. A recent refurbishment has made the interior bright and contemporary, and in winter months it is a cosy retreat, serving draught beers and real ales. Facilities include wifi, a pool table and a big screen showing live sporting fixtures.

The Fair View Inn

Burnedge, Rochdale, Greater Manchester OL16 4QQ • Tel: 01706 645517

This distinguished looking two-storey inn is situated on the main road between Rochdale and Shaw, and enjoys breathtaking views over surrounding counties. It is furnished to a high standard, and customers can sample the popular roast dinners, accompanied by a glass of fine wine or ale.

Scotland • Regions

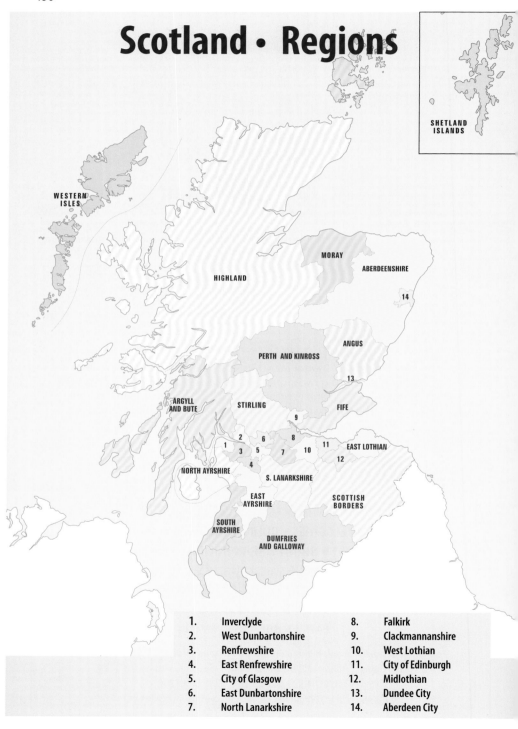

SHETLAND ISLANDS

WESTERN ISLES

MORAY

ABERDEENSHIRE

HIGHLAND

14

ANGUS

PERTH AND KINROSS

13

ARGYLL AND BUTE

STIRLING

FIFE

9

2

6

8

1

3

5

7

10

11

EAST LOTHIAN

4

12

NORTH AYRSHIRE

S. LANARKSHIRE

EAST AYRSHIRE

SCOTTISH BORDERS

SOUTH AYRSHIRE

DUMFRIES AND GALLOWAY

1.	Inverclyde	8.	Falkirk
2.	West Dunbartonshire	9.	Clackmannanshire
3.	Renfrewshire	10.	West Lothian
4.	East Renfrewshire	11.	City of Edinburgh
5.	City of Glasgow	12.	Midlothian
6.	East Dunbartonshire	13.	Dundee City
7.	North Lanarkshire	14.	Aberdeen City

Scotland

Well Country Inn, Scotlandwell, Kinross, p154

Kildrummy Inn, Alford, Aberdeenshire, p140

Creggans Inn, Loch Fyne, Argyll, p145

Aberdeen, Banff & Moray

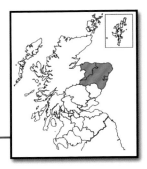

Angus & Dundee

The Bell Tree

Panmurefield Road, Broughty Ferry, Dundee, Angus DD5 3TS
Tel: 01382 738112

A contemporary establishment situated in Broughty Ferry, with a Chef & Brewer-style menu and a traditional interior with real log fires and little nooks. A wide range of whiskies, real ales and beers is available. Accommodation is at the adjacent Premier Inn where 60 en suite bedrooms have all modern facilities.

Argyll & Bute

RATES

Normal Bed & Breakfast rate per person **(single room)**		Normal Bed & Breakfast rate per person **(sharing double/twin room)**	
PRICE RANGE	CATEGORY	PRICE RANGE	CATEGORY
Under £35	S£	Under £35	D£
£36-£45	S££	£36-£45	D££
£46-£55	S£££	£46-£55	D£££
Over £55	S££££	Over £55	D££££

This is meant as an indication only and does not show prices for Special Breaks, Weekends, etc. Guests are therefore advised to verify all prices on enquiring or booking.

ARGYLL & BUTE is a wonderfully unspoilt area, historically the heartland of Scotland and home to a wealth of fascinating wildlife. Here you may be lucky enough to catch a glimpse of an eagle, a wildcat or an osprey, or even a fine antlered stag. At every step the sea fringed landscape is steeped in history, from prehistoric sculpture at Kilmartin, to the elegant ducal home of the once feared Clan Campbell. There are also reminders of pre-historic times with Bronze Age cup-and-ring engravings, and standing stone circles. On the upper reaches of Loch Caolisport can be found St Columba's Cave, and more recent times are illustrated at the Auchindrain Highland Township south of Inveraray, a friendly little town with plenty to see, including the Jail, Wildlife Park and Maritime Museum.

Bute is the most accessible of the west coast islands, and Rothesay is its main town. Explore the dungeons and grand hall of Rothesay Castle, or visit the fascinating Bute Museum. The town offers a full range of leisure facilities, including a fine swimming pool and superb golf course, and there are vast areas of parkland where youngsters can safely play.

West Loch Hotel

By Tarbert
Loch Fyne
Argyll
PA29 6YF

Tel: 01880 820283
Fax: 01880 820930

An attractive, family-run, 18th century coaching inn of character, the West Loch Hotel is well situated for a relaxing holiday. It is renowned for outstanding food. After dining, guests can relax in front of an open fire, perhaps sampling some of the local malt whiskies. With glorious scenery, the area is excellent for hill-walking and enjoying the wide variety of wildlife. Visits to Islay, Jura, Arran and Gigha can be pleasant day trips, and attractions in the area include castles, distilleries, gardens and sandy beaches. Fishing, golf and boat hire are all available locally.

www.westlochhotel.co.uk • e-mail: westlochhotel@btinternet.com

8 BEDROOMS, ALL EN SUITE/WITH PRIVATE BATHROOM. CHILDREN AND PETS WELCOME.
BAR AND RESTAURANT MEALS. INVERARAY 62 MILES.

Visit the FHG website

www.holidayguides.com

for details of the wide choice of accommodation

featured in the full range of FHG titles

FREE or REDUCED RATE entry to Holiday Visits and Attractions –
see our READERS' OFFER VOUCHERS on pages 187-218

Borders

Covering about eighteen hundred miles, **The Scottish Borders** stretch from the rolling hills and moorland in the west, through gentler valleys to the rich agricultural plains of the east, and the rocky Berwickshire coastline with its secluded coves and picturesque fishing villages. Through the centre, tracing a silvery course from the hills to the sea, runs the River Tweed which provides some of the best fishing in Scotland. As well as fishing there is golf – 18 courses in all, riding or cycling and some of the best modern sports centres and swimming pools in the country. Friendly towns and charming villages are there to be discovered, while castles, abbeys, stately homes and museums illustrate the exciting and often bloody history of the area. It's this history which is commemorated in the Common Ridings and other local festivals, creating a colourful pageant much enjoyed by visitors and native Borderers alike.

One of the delights of travelling is finding gifts and keepsakes with a genuine local flavour, and dedicated souvenir hunters will find a plentiful supply of traditional delicacies, from drinks to baking and handmade sweets. Handcrafted jewellery, pottery, glass and woodwork, as well as beautiful tweeds and high quality knitwear can be found in the many interesting little shops throughout the area.

Scottish Borders eating establishments take pride in providing particularly good food and service and the choice of hotels, inns restaurants and cafes make eating out a real pleasure.

Edinburgh & Lothians

Jusinlees Inn

Esbank Toll, Dalkeith, Midlothian EH22 3AT • Tel: 0131 6632166

Prominently positioned on the roundabout in Dalkeith is this colossal white building with a beautifully traditional interior. With a circular centre bar and open plan layout, patrons may drink or dine where they choose. Amenities include free wifi, plasma screens, a large TV screen, pool table, dart board, and a beer garden.

IGLU (Bar & Ethical Eaterie)

2b Jamaica Street, Edinburgh, Midlothian EH3 6HH
Tel: 0131 476 5333 • www.theiglu.com/

Try food and drink from a different direction! Edinburgh is home to many fine establishments but none as special as this. Since the addition of a food service in 2005, its popularity has gone from strength to strength, offering all your favourite alcoholic beverages including cocktails.

THE MALT SHOVEL

11-15 Cockburn Street, Edinburgh, Lothians EH1 1BP • Tel: 01312 256 843

This charming public house is located between the Royal Mile and the railway station. The interior is furnished in old dark wood, from the picture frames and fireplaces to the beams and flooring, with original stained glass on the doors. The pub boasts the biggest selection (105!) of malt whiskies in the area, plus well kept real ales. With haggis on the menu and live entertainment, this is definitely worth a visit!

The Shakespeare

65 Lothian Road, Edinburgh, Lothians EH1 2DJ • Tel: 0131 2288400

The Shakespeare is one of Edinburgh's best-known and oldest pubs, and its location in the centre of the city means that it attracts a remarkably cosmopolitan crowd. Food is served throughout the day and live sporting fixtures are shown on an extra-large screen. Entertainment includes a weekly quiz and fortnightly karaoke.

The Rose Street Brewery

55 Rose Street, Edinburgh, Lothians EH2 2NH • Tel: 0131 2201227

The Rose was once a brewery, but is now a lively social centre on famous cobbled Rose Street in Edinburgh. Having undergone a recent refurbishment, the colour scheme is now an elegant blend of creams, browns and burgundy. Attractions include a great wine list and a range of dishes cooked to order – steaks are very popular here!

Hopetoun Inn

8 McDonald Road, Edinburgh, Lothians EH7 4LU

Tel: 0131 5583523 • Fax: 0131 5587338 • www.hopetouninn.co.uk

Regulars enjoy live sporting fixtures shown on a large screen, but that's not the only reason for coming to the Hopetoun. The facilities are great, with a pool table and dart boards, plus weekly entertainment such as a quiz, karaoke and live bands.

The Lady Nairne

228 Willowbrae Road, Edinburgh, Lothians EH8 7NG • Tel: 0131 6613396

The perfect venue for a stag or hen weekend, The Lady Nairne is located just three miles from Edinburgh city centre. There is an extensive à la carte menu, with a good choice of wines as the perfect accompaniment. Accommodation is in 39 en suite bedrooms, all with modern facilities.

THE BALMWELL

39/41 Howden Hall Road, Edinburgh, Lothians EH16 6PG

Tel: 0131 6721408 • Fax: 0131 6661271

Lovers of wildlife can expect to see squirrels and foxes running about in the extensive gardens of this former convent. With a Two For One meal deals on delicious food and a wide range of wines from around the world, there's something for everyone.

The Cuddie Brae

Newcraighall, Edinburgh, Lothians EH21 8SG • Tel: 01316 571212

This Chef & Brewer pub venue is situated opposite the railway station, just five miles from the city centre. The interior is contemporary in style and the menu features mouth-watering dishes prepared from fresh ingredients. Accommodation is in 42 rooms, all en suite, with modern facilities.

The Granary

Almondvale Boulevard, Livingston, West Lothian EH54 6QT

Tel: 01506 410661 • Fax: 01506 415027

Purpose-built building located next to the Arndale Centre, offering great value for money and a comfortable environment in which to relax, dine and enjoy a glass of your favourite wine. The regulars are a friendly bunch who enjoy the weekly entertainment.

Fife

The Smugglers Inn

High Street East, Anstruther, Fife KY10 3DQ
Tel: 01333 310506 • Fax: 01333 312706
You cannot miss The Smugglers – an attractive inn situated on High Street East in Anstruther. Overlooking the old harbour, it is idyllically placed for fishing, bird watching, golf and sightseeing. The bar is stocked with a wide range of draught beers, real ales and malt whiskies, and the en suite accommodation is cosy and comfortable.

The Ceres Inn

The Cross, Ceres, Fife KY15 5NE
Tel: 01334 828 305 • www.ceresinn.co.uk
Newly renovated and under new ownership is this bistro inn in Fife. The entire restaurant may be hired out for special occasions, and the regular pub area stocks a remarkable selection of real ales and 80 varieties of whisky! Entertainment includes live music and karaoke.

The Auld Hoose

8 Nethergate, Kinghorn, Fife KY3 9SY
Tel: 01592 891074 • Fax: 01592 891367
The Auld Hoose is listed in the Good Beer Guide and is a firm favourite in Fife. For those in search of some peace and quiet, this family-run establishment is ideal, with a wide range of beers, real ales and lagers as well as over 30 malt whiskies. Self-catering accommodation with two double and one twin bedrooms is available to let.

Family-Friendly
Pubs, Inns & Hotels
See the Supplement on pages 183-186 for establishments which really welcome children

Highlands

Inn at Dalwhinnie
Dalwhinnie, Inverness-shire PH19 1AG
Tel: 01528 522257 • room@theinndalwhinnie.com • www.theinndalwhinnie.com
The Dalwhinnie provides guests with maximum comfort and offers lots of information on things to do and see. With live music and an abundance of traditional and modern fish dishes on the menu, it's an ideal spot to leave your troubles behind. All rooms are en suite and spacious with beautiful window views. Great selection of malt whiskies.

THE BEN NEVIS BAR
103 High Street, Fort William, Inverness-shire PH33 6DG • Tel: 01397 702295
Formerly this was the inn for the castle drovers; today, having undergone a contemporary makeover, the establishment exudes style and panache. The bar is split across two levels, with a restaurant upstairs affording stunning views. Enjoy a glass of fine wine on the new decking area overlooking the loch.

The Fluke
Culcabock Road, Inverness, Inverness-shire IV2 3XQ • Tel: 01463 220957
The Fluke is an ideal spot in which to dine, drink and celebrate the victory of your favourite football team, with live fixtures shown regularly on big screens. Facilities include a pool table, dart board and two large alcoves for private functions.

The Old Inn
Flowerdale, Gairloch, Ross-shire IV21 2BD
Tel: 01445 712006 • Fax: 01445 712445
Perfectly positioned by the harbour in Gairloch, and popular with local fishermen who appreciate the wholesome food that is served. A good selection of draught beers and real ales is offered behind the bar, and accommodation is available in well equipped bedrooms.

Perth & Kinross

YANN'S AT GLENEARN HOUSE (on facing page)

5 BEDROOMS, ALL WITH PRIVATE BATHROOM. ALL BEDROOMS NON-SMOKING. FREE HOUSE. CHILDREN AND PETS WELCOME. RESTAURANT MEALS WED-SUN. PERTH 16 MILES. S£££, D££££.

Yann's at Glenearn House

is a family-owned business, with Yannick and Shari Grospellier as your hosts.

Glenearn is a large Victorian house in the picturesque town of Crieff, in Perthshire. It has recently been refurbished and now features a restaurant with rooms with a great relaxed atmosphere where you can eat, drink and sleep.

Crieff is known as the Gateway to the Highlands and is a perfect, central location for discovering Scotland, only an hour's drive from Edinburgh and Glasgow. Golf courses are plentiful, ranging from Crieff's two 18-hole courses to the renowned Gleneagles courses, only 8 miles away.

At Yann's, cooking is a passion, The emphasis is on good food, kept simple and traditional, and we aim to make you feel at home in our relaxed and convivial bistro. A relaxed and welcoming lounge awaits you for pre-dinner drinks and coffee or digestifs.

We have five spacious bedrooms (double or twin), all decorated in their own unique style and each with an en suite shower room or adjoining bathroom.

Each bedroom features home-from-home luxuries such as digital television, hi-fi, DVD, tea and coffee-making facilities and quality toiletries.

Yann's at Glenearn House

Glenearn House, Perth Road, Crieff, Perthshire PH7 3EQ

Tel: 01764 650111

e-mail: info@yannsatglenearnhouse.com

www.yannsatglenearnhouse.com

Stirling & The Trossachs

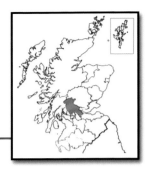

Behind The Wall

14 Melville Street, Falkirk, Stirlingshire FK1 1HZ

Tel: 01324633338 • www.behindthewall.co.uk

The radical way to live! Anything goes here at Behind The Wall, who proclaim that they 'make their own rules and then bend them'. This bar, eatery and entertainment venue is open all day and is ideal for the whole family, including young children. Facilities include an outdoor area and conservatory; wifi throughout.

The Rosebank

Main Street, Camelon, Falkirk, Stirlingshire FK1 4DS

Tel: 01324 611842 • Fax: 01324 617154

This prestigious Listed building is located in the small village of Camelon, beside the Forth and Clyde Canal between Edinburgh and Glasgow, and stands on the site of a former whisky distillery. Now a bar and 200-cover restaurant, it is ideal for a relaxing meal with friends or family.

The Outside Inn

Bellsdyke Road, Larbert, Stirlingshire FK5 4EG • Tel: 01324 579411

A newly refurbished inn, particularly popular with business people, shoppers and family diners. Original features include waterfalls and paths running through the indoor space; in summer, take advantage of the attractive beer garden. Facilities include wifi throughout and a smoking shelter.

RATES   S – SINGLE ROOM rate   D – Sharing DOUBLE/TWIN ROOM

S£ D£ =Under £35   S££ D££ =£36-£45   S£££ D£££ =£46-£55   S££££ D££££ =Over £55

This is meant as an indication only and does not show prices for Special Breaks, Weekends, etc. Guests are therefore advised to verify all prices on enquiring or booking.

Scottish Islands

Isle of Mull

THE BELLACHROY
The Oldest Inn on Mull — Est. 1608 —

e-mail: info@thebellachroy.co.uk
www.thebellachroy.co.uk

*The Bellachroy is the oldest Inn on Mull,
an historic drovers' Inn renowned for quality home cooked food,
where you will receive a warm welcome and genuine hospitality.*
- 6 en suite bedrooms and characterful bars.
- Stunning location for exploring and touring.
- Open all year round • Well behaved dogs welcome.

The Bellachroy, Dervaig, Isle of Mull PA75 6QW • Tel: 01688 400314

6 BEDROOMS, ALL WITH PRIVATE BATHROOM. FREE HOUSE WITH REAL ALE. CHILDREN AND PETS WELCOME.
BAR MEALS/SNACKS AFTERNOONS ONLY, RESTAURANT OPEN LUNCH/DINNER. ALL PUBLIC AREAS NON-SMOKING.
TOBERMORY 5 MILES. S£££, D££.

RATES

Normal Bed & Breakfast rate per person **(single room)**		Normal Bed & Breakfast rate per person **(sharing double/twin room)**	
PRICE RANGE	CATEGORY	PRICE RANGE	CATEGORY
Under £35	S£	Under £35	D£
£36-£45	S££	£36-£45	D££
£46-£55	S£££	£46-£55	D£££
Over £55	S££££	Over £55	D££££

This is meant as an indication only and does not show prices for Special Breaks,
Weekends, etc. Guests are therefore advised to verify all prices on enquiring or booking.

Isle of Skye

Since the 1700s this solid white-washed hotel has gazed over the Sound of Sleat to the Knoydart Mountains and the beautiful Sands of Morar, and as well as being one of the oldest coaching inns on the west coast, it is surely one of the most idyllically situated.

Not surprisingly, seafood features extensively on the menu here, together with local venison and other fine Scottish produce, and tasty bar lunches and suppers are offered as an alternative to the more formal cuisine served in the restaurant.

A private residents' lounge is furnished to the same high standard of comfort as the cosy guest rooms, all of which have private facilities.

ARDVASAR HOTEL
Ardvasar, Sleat, Isle of Skye IV45 8RS
Tel: 01471 844223 • Fax: 01471 844495
www.ardvasarhotel.com
e-mail: richard@ardvasar-hotel.demon.co.uk

10 BEDROOMS, ALL WITH PRIVATE BATHROOM. ALL BEDROOMS NON-SMOKING. FREE HOUSE WITH REAL ALE. CHILDREN AND PETS WELCOME. BAR MEALS AND RESTAURANT MEALS. BROADFORD 16 MILES. S££££, D££££.

Visit the FHG website
www.holidayguides.com
for details of the wide choice of accommodation
featured in the full range of FHG titles

FREE or REDUCED RATE entry to Holiday Visits and Attractions –
see our **READERS' OFFER VOUCHERS** on pages 187-218

Ratings & Awards

For the first time ever the AA, VisitBritain, VisitScotland, and the Wales Tourist Board will use a single method of assessing and rating serviced accommodation. Irrespective of which organisation inspects an establishment the rating awarded will be the same, using a common set of standards, giving a clear guide of what to expect. The RAC is no longer operating an Hotel inspection and accreditation business.

Accommodation Standards: Star Grading Scheme

Using a scale of 1-5 stars the objective quality ratings give a clear indication of accommodation standard, cleanliness, ambience, hospitality, service and food, This shows the full range of standards suitable for every budget and preference, and allows visitors to distinguish between the quality of accommodation and facilities on offer in different establishments. All types of board and self-catering accommodation are covered, including hotels, B&Bs, holiday parks, campus accommodation, hostels, caravans and camping, and boats.

VisitBritain and the regional tourist boards, enjoyEngland.com, VisitScotland and VisitWales, and the AA have full details of the grading system on their websites

The more stars, the higher level of quality

★★★★★
exceptional quality, with a degree of luxury

★★★★
excellent standard throughout

★★★
very good level of quality and comfort

★★
good quality, well presented and well run

★
acceptable quality; simple, practical, no frills

National Accessible Scheme

If you have particular mobility, visual or hearing needs, look out for the National Accessible Scheme. You can be confident of finding accommodation or attractions that meet your needs by looking for the following symbols.

 Typically suitable for a person with sufficient mobility to climb a flight of steps but would benefit from fixtures and fittings to aid balance

 Typically suitable for a person with restricted walking ability and for those that may need to use a wheelchair some of the time and can negotiate a maximum of three steps

 Typically suitable for a person who depends on the use of a wheelchair and transfers unaided to and from the wheelchair in a seated position. This person may be an independent traveller

 Typically suitable for a person who depends on the use of a wheelchair in a seated position. This person also requires personal or mechanical assistance (eg carer, hoist).

Wales

The Crown Inn, Rhadayer, Powys, p172

The Hand at Llanarmon, Llangollen, North Wales, p165

Trewern Arms Hotel, Newport, Pembrokeshire, p171

Anglesey & Gwynedd

North Wales

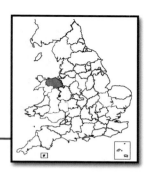

The White Horse Inn

The Square, Cilcain, Mold, North Wales CH7 5NN • Tel: 01352 740142

Located on the slope of Moel Fammau in North Wales, an area of outstanding natural beauty. Homemade bar meals are prepared fresh to order, and the bar is stocked with a choice of real ales, draught beers, lagers and wines. The pub is especially popular with walkers, cyclists and horse riders. Children over 14 years are welcome.

THE HARBOUR

Foryd Road, Rhyl, North Wales LL18 5BA • Tel: 01745 360644

The Harbour can be found just over the bridge in the little town of Rhyl. The building is attractively decorated inside and out, with comfortable fittings and furnishings, and the bar is well stocked with draught beers, spirits, ales and wines. Sample one of the pub's hearty meals which are available at most reasonable prices.

The Grapes Inn

Francis Road, Moss, Wrexham, North Wales LL11 6EB • Tel: 01978 720585

A free house with a homely interior made up of wooden furnishings, an open log fire and family artefacts including a collection of 250 jugs on beamed shelving. Beers, real ales, wines, spirits and whiskies are available - and don't forget to try the delicious grills with chips and vegetables. Facilities include a beer garden, pool table and jukebox.

The Black Horse

Hall Street, Penycae, Wrexham, North Wales LL14 2RU • Tel: 01978 840796

A pint at the Black Horse comes with the guarantee of exceptional views over Llangollen and Castle Dinas Brian. It is situated on the edge of Penycae, just a short walk to the lakes and reservoirs, and popular with hikers, walkers, and cyclists. Food is served throughout the day. Regular entertainment includes live music, karaoke, discos and DJs.

Carmarthenshire

The Prince of Wales Inn
Mynyddygarreg, Kidwelly, Carmarthenshire SA17 4RP • Tel: 01554 890522
This free house boasts six of its own real ales as well as several other Welsh ones and one real cider – all on tap! The size of the pub helps create a cosy, intimate ambience, with a log fire and interesting artefacts and memorabilia throughout.

The Phoenix
Penygroes Road, Gorslas, Llanelli, Carmarthenshire SA14 7LA • Tel: 01269 844438
The Phoenix is set in the rural village of Gorslas, a regular ramblers' haunt. The bar is stocked with a wide range of lagers, beers and wines and is the only public house in the village where food is served. The menu is imaginative and all dishes are prepared from fresh ingredients. Regular entertainment includes 60s/70s nights, quiz nights and themed food evenings.

The Thomas Arms Hotel
Thomas Street, Llanelli, Carmarthenshire SA15 3JF • Tel: 01554 772043
Having undergone a major refurbishment, the pub now boasts a unique atmosphere, with a neutral colour scheme and homely fixtures and furnishings. This is the ideal spot for a relaxing drink after a hard day at work or for a family lunch or dinner. Accommodation is in ten en suite bedrooms with all modern facilities.

THE STRADEY ARMS
1 Stradey Road, Furnace, Llanelli, Carmarthenshire SA15 4ET
Tel: 01554 757968
For a quiet drink or meal, pop in to the Stradey Arms, located in the heart of the village of Furnace. Regular attractions include a weekly quiz, a large beer garden, a plasma screen and free wifi throughout.

The Coopers Arms

Station Road, Newcastle Emlyn, Carmarthenshire SA38 9BX • Tel: 01239 710323
Located just outside the town, with panoramic views of the remains of the Norman castle and the River Teifi. The bar stocks a wide selection of draught ales, beers and fine wines. Homemade meals include steaks and a vegetarian option.

The Black Horse

Iscoed Road, Hendy, Pontarddulais, Carmarthenshire SA4 0UN • Tel: 01792 882239
The small village of Hendy boasts a friendly community who regard the charming Black Horse pub as a home-from-home. With wooden beams and open fires, the pub serves a variety of mouth-watering dishes, all of which go down beautifully with a pint of real ale!

The Salutation Inn

Pontargothi, Nantgaredig, Carmarthenshire SA32 7NH • Tel: 01267 290336
The extensive menu at this beautiful inn offers a range of meals to suit all palates, including tasty pizzas made from scratch. Its location makes it the perfect stop off point for walkers and fishermen. Dogs are welcome at this establishment.

The Savoy Country Inn

Tenby Road, St Clears, Carmarthenshire SA33 4JP • Tel: 01994 230664
A secluded country inn in the heart of the beautiful scenery of West Wales. The interior is pleasingly traditional, with low ceilings, and a mix of armchairs and sofas. Facilities include a games room, pool table and dart board, and an indoor amusement arcade. En suite bedrooms provide overnight accommodation.

RATES

Normal Bed & Breakfast rate per person
(single room)

PRICE RANGE	CATEGORY
Under £35	S£
£36-£45	S££
£46-£55	S£££
Over £55	S££££

Normal Bed & Breakfast rate per person
(sharing double/twin room)

PRICE RANGE	CATEGORY
Under £35	D£
£36-£45	D££
£46-£55	D£££
Over £55	D££££

This is meant as an indication only and does not show prices for Special Breaks, Weekends, etc. Guests are therefore advised to verify all prices on enquiring or booking.

Ceredigion

The Monachty

Market Street, Aberaeron, Ceredigion SA46 0AS • Tel: 01545 570389

Situated next to the harbour on the busy main street in Aberaeron is this refurbished pub venue, offering guests superb views as they dine and drink. After a deliciously filling meal, why not relax in one of the big armchairs or sofas in the lounge downstairs. Accommodation is in seven en suite bedrooms with a full range of facilities including tea/coffee-making.

The Lord Beechings

Alexandra Road, Aberystwyth, Ceredigion SY23 1LE • Tel: 01970 625069

Aberystwyth is a university town and this large pub venue is a student favourite. Order food at the contemporary bar and relax with a pint of guest ale in a comfy chair while it is cooked to your liking. Facilities include free wifi.

THE WHITE LION HOTEL

Talybont, Aberystwyth, Ceredigion SY24 5ER • Tel: 01970 832245

Homely, family-run hotel set just a short distance from the beaches and Ynflaf Nature Reserve, popular with walkers, cyclists and fishermen. It makes an ideal stop off for a pint and some delicious pub food, with attractive original features such as a slate floor, ceiling hooks and an old fireplace. Two twin, two double and one family bedroom each have freeview TV and coffee/tea making facilities.

The Black Lion Hotel

Pontrhydfendigaid, Ystrad Meurig, Ceredigion SY25 6BE
Tel: 01974 831624 • Fax: 01974 831052 • www.blacklionhotel.co.uk

Located only 20 minutes from Aberystwyth is this cosy, comfortable pub hotel, ideal for a walking holiday, with many walkways, cycle paths and nature trails to explore. There is a stylish bar and restaurant, plus five en suite bedrooms, each with modern facilities.

The Miners Arms

Pontrhyd-y-groes, Ystrad Meurig, Ceredigion SY25 6DN • Tel: 01974 282238

Situated in the tranquil Ystwyth Valley is this delightful inn – the last remaining pub out of five in the village of Pontrhyd-y-groes. The pub has built a great reputation for serving outstanding homemade specials including meat, fish and vegetarian dishes. A good range of draught beers, real ale and fine wines is stocked. B&B accommodation available.

The Ship Inn

Tresaith, Cardigan, Ceredigion SA43 2JL • Tel: 01239 811816

Tresaith is a quaint little coastal village with popular beaches and one pub – the Ship Inn. Patrons can relax and enjoy stunning views of the sea, and food is served throughout the day at reasonable prices. Accommodation is in four en suite rooms with colour TV.

THE THREE HORSESHOES INN

Llangeitho, Tregaron, Ceredigion SY25 6TW • Tel: 01974 821244

Set in the rural heart of West Wales is this family-run pub with a large beer garden, a games room and a takeaway food service. All dishes are home-made and prepared from fresh ingredients. The bar offers a good selection of ales, draught beers and fine wines .

THE BLACK LION HOTEL

High Street, Lampeter, Ceredigion SA48 7BG • Tel: 01570 422172

Set in the university market town of Lampeter is this former courthouse with a traditional pub interior, comfy armchairs and wooden fittings and furnishings. The beer garden is perfect for alfresco dining in summer months. Accommodation is in 18 bedrooms, all en suite, with coffee/tea making facilities.

Family-Friendly
Pubs, Inns & Hotels

See the Supplement on pages 183-186 for establishments which really welcome children

FREE or REDUCED RATE entry to Holiday Visits and Attractions –
see our **READERS' OFFER VOUCHERS** on pages 187-218

Pembrokeshire

Powys

South Wales

Pet-Friendly Pubs

The Bell Inn, Adderbury, Oxfordshire

The Hood Arms, Kilve, Somerset

A selection of Pubs and Inns where pets are especially welcome!

The Greyhound

Eton Wick, Berkshire SL4 6JE • Tel: 01753 863925
www.thegreyhoundetonwick.co.uk
A picturesque pub with plenty of walks close by. Food served daily. Sunday lunch only £5.95 between 12 noon – 3pm.
Pet residents: Tully (Shepherd), Harvey (Retriever), Teeni, Bourbon.

The Springer Spaniel

Treburley, near Launceston, Cornwall PL15 9NS
Tel: 01579 370424 • e-mail: enquiries@thespringerspaniel.org.uk
www.thespringerspaniel.org.uk
Country pub providing a warm welcome and specialising in home cooked, fresh, locally sourced food. Emphasis upon game, with beef and lamb from the owner's organic farm. Dogs can snooze by the fire, water provided (perhaps a biscuit if especially good) or lounge in the beer garden.
Pet Regulars: some very regular customers and their accompanying owners.

Cumberland Inn   Tel: 01434 381875

Townfoot, Alston, Cumbria CA9 3HX
stay@cumberlandinnalston.com • www.cumberlandinnalston.com
A comfy retreat in the secluded North Pennines. Real beer, real fires and real hospitality await your arrival. Home-made hearty fare available all day to revive flagging spirits. Our 5 recently refurbished rooms are all en suite. Muddy dogs and boots welcome.
Dog bowls filled with water (or even beer).
Pets welcome in bedrooms and bar. No charge for pets.

the mardale inn @ st patrick's well

Bampton, Cumbria CA10 2RQ Tel: 01931 713244
www.mardaleinn.co.uk info@mardaleinn.co.uk
Always open • fresh local produce • open fires
fine cask beers • warm beds • Haweswater location.
Daily Telegraph '50 Best Pubs' - May 2008.
Children and dogs welcome
(children must be kept on a short leash at all times!)

Three Horseshoes

Powerstock, Bridport, Dorset DT6 3TF • 01308 485328
info@threehorseshoesinn.com
www.threehorseshoesinn.com

'The Shoes' is a Victorian inn tucked away in a peaceful part of West Dorset. The Inn boasts a great reputation for excellent cuisine. An à la carte menu with specials board is served daily, plus lunchtime snacks. Dogs and children welcome.
Pets welcome in bar, garden and accommodation.
Pet Residents: JJ and Piglet. Pet Regular: Guinness

The White Swan

The Square, 31 High Street, Swanage, Dorset BH19 2LJ • 01929 423804
e-mail: info@whiteswanswanage.co.uk • www.whiteswanswanage.co.uk

A pub with a warm and friendly atmosphere, three minutes from the beach. Traditional pub food, Sunday roasts. Large beer garden. En suite accommodation with parking. Free wifi and internet access. TV and pool table. Children and dogs welcome.
Water, treats • Dogs allowed in beer garden, bar area and accommodation.
Pet resident: Bagsy (Sharpei). Regulars: Meg, Liddy and Em (Black Labradors), Sally and Sophie (Jack Russells), Ruby (English Bulldog), Patch (Jack Russell), Prince (King Charles Spaniel.

The Silent Woman Inn

Bere Road, Coldharbour, Wareham, Dorset BH20 7PA
Tel: 01929 552909 • www.thesilentwoman.co.uk

Traditional country inn nestling in the heart of Wareham Forest. Beautiful gardens, log fires in winter. All fresh ingredients, wonderful food. Real ales, good wines. Adults-only inside.
Water bowls and treats - and affection • Dogs allowed in bar areas and all outside areas except children's play areas.
Pet Residents: Rosie and Ellie (Labs). Regulars: Bruno, Tilly and many others.

The Square & Compasses

Fuller Street, Fairstead, Essex CM3 2BB • 01245 361477
info@thesquareandcompasses.co.uk • www.thesquareandcompasses.co.uk

Independently owned 17thC freehouse in a small sleepy village surrounded by picturesque countryside and near Essex Way long distance footpath. Only a short drive from new Great Leighs racecourse. Food is simple and straightforward, with daily changing chalkboard menus and traditional classic dishes, freshly prepared using local produce. Private dining room. Real ales. Garden and terrace.
Dogs welcome in bar area and garden. Water bowl available.

The Whalebone Freehouse

Chapel Road, Fingringhoe, Colchester, Essex CO5 7BG
Tel/Fax: 01206 729307 • e-mail: fburroughes307@aol.com

Only minutes from Colchester, the Whalebone offers a wide range of excellent food and real ales. Pets are most welcome inside the pub and in the beer garden. Excellent dog-walking trails in and around Fingringhoe. Water bowls provided on request.
Pet Residents: Rosie and Poppy (Basset Hounds)

The Tunnel House Inn

Coates, Cirencester, Gloucestershire GL7 6PW • 01285 770280
e-mail: bookings@tunnelhouse.com • www.tunnelhouse.com

A traditional Cotswold pub set on the edge of a wood. The perfect haven for pets, families, in fact everyone. Home-cooked pub food, traditional ales and ciders. Endless walks lead off from the pub in all directions.
Pets are welcome in all areas inside and out
Plenty of space; water and occasional treats provided.
Pet Regulars: Madge, very friendly Patterdale terrier - loves other dogs too!

The Broadway

112 London Road, East Grinstead, West Sussex RH19 1EP
Tel: 01342 410306 • e-mail: the-broadway@btconnect.com
www.myspace.com/thebroadwayeg

The Broadway is a large town centre pub, where you will always receive a warm welcome from our friendly staff. Two real ales on tap; Cask Marque accredited. Large front patio with car park at rear of pub.
Well behaved dogs on leash allowed in pub at any time of day.

The Lamb Inn

High Street, Hindon, Wiltshire SP3 6DP
Tel: 01747 820573 • Fax: 01747 820605
www.lambathindon.co.uk

12th Century historic inn with bedrooms full of character.
Outstanding food and great wine selection.
Pets welcome in the bar and bedrooms. ETC/AA ★★★★

The Castle Inn

7 Wistowgate, Cawood
Selby, North Yorkshire YO8 3SH
Tel: 01757 268324
info@castleinncawood.co.uk • www.castleinncawood.co.uk

18thC village pub with a 60-seat restaurant and an 18-pitch caravan site. All food is local and fresh.
Water bowls outside.
Pet Resident: Elvis (9-year old Springer Spaniel)

Old Hall Inn

Tel: 01756 752441
Main Street, Threshfield, Grassington, N, Yorks BD23 5HB
oldhallinn@fsmail.net • www.oldhallinnandcottages.co.uk

18thC Inn, renowned for fine ales and award-winning cuisine.
Large beer garden. Children's outdoor play area. B&B in four en suite bedrooms; quality self-catering available in adjacent cottages.
Well behaved dogs welcome.

Simonstone Hall

Hawes, North Yorkshire DL8 3LY
Tel: 01969 667255 • www.simonstonehall.com

Welcoming bar with great atmosphere.
Wide range of bar meals from snacks to Sunday Lunch.
Comfortable accommodation.
Dogs of all shapes sizes and breeds welcome.

The West Arms Hotel

Llanarmon Dyffryn Ceiriog, Nr Llangollen, Denbighshire
North Wales LL20 7LF • Tel: 01691 600665
e-mail: gowestarms@aol.com • www.thewestarms.co.uk

16th century Hotel full of charm and character. Award winning restaurant, bar meals lunchtime and evening.
En suite bedrooms. Welcome pets.

Ballachulish Hotel

Ballachulish, Argyll PA39 4JY
Tel: 01855 811606 • www.ballachulishhotel.com

Stay, refuel, relax and refresh in this historic hotel in a lochside setting. Bar and Bistro serving market fresh produce. Dogs allowed in the lounge and guests' bedrooms, excluding food areas.

THE MUNRO INN

Strathyre, Perthshire FK18 8NA• Tel: 01877 384333
www.munro-inn.com

Chilled out Robbie warmly welcomes doggy friends to the Munro Inn in beautiful Highland Perthshire. Perfect base for walking, cycling, climbing, water sports, fishing or relaxing! Great home cooking, lively bar, luxurious en suite bedrooms, drying room, broadband internet.

Four Seasons Hotel

St Fillans, Perthshire • Tel: 01764 685333

Hotel in picturesque setting offering comfortable bedrooms, chalets and apartment. Fine dining restaurant and bar. Dogs allowed in all non-food areas.

Looking for Holiday Accommodation?

FHG
K·U·P·E·R·A·R·D

for details of hundreds of properties throughout the UK, visit our website

www.holidayguides.com

Family-Friendly Pubs & Inns

This is a selection of establishments which make an extra effort to cater for parents and children. The majority provide a separate children's menu or they may be willing to serve small portions of main course dishes on request; there are often separate outdoor or indoor play areas where the junior members of the family can let off steam while Mum and Dad unwind over a drink.

NB: Not all of the establishments featured here have a listing in the main section of this book.

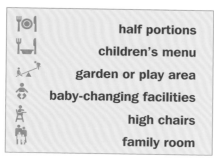

half portions

children's menu

garden or play area

baby-changing facilities

high chairs

family room

THE WELLINGTON ARMS

203 Yorktown Road, Sandhurst,
Berkshire GU47 9BN
Tel: 01252 872408
www.thewellingtonarms.co.uk

VICTORIA INN

Perranuthnoe, Near Penzance,
Cornwall TR20 9NP
Tel: 01736 710309
www.victoriainn-penzance.co.uk

CROOKED INN

Stoketon Cross, Trematon,
Saltash, Cornwall PL12 4RZ
Tel: 01752 848177
www.crooked-inn.co.uk

KINGS ARMS HOTEL

Hawkshead, Ambleside,
Cumbria LA22 0NZ
Tel: 015394 36372
www.kingsarmshawkshead.co.uk

EAGLE & CHILD INN

Kendal Road, Staveley,
Cumbria LA8 9LP
Tel: 01539 821320
www.eaglechildinn.co.uk

MARDALE INN
St Patrick's Well, Bampton,
Cumbria CA19 2RQ
Tel: 01931 713244
www.mardaleinn.co.uk

GILPIN BRIDGE
Bridge End, Levens,
Near Kendal, Cumbria LA8 8EP
Tel: 015395 52206
www.gilpinbridgeinn.co.uk

GREYHOUND HOTEL
Main Street, Shap, Penrith,
Cumbria CA10 3PW
Tel: 01931 716474
www.greyhoundshap.co.uk

QUEEN'S HEAD
Main Street, Hawkshead,
Cumbria LA22 0NS
Tel: 015394 36271
www.queensheadhotel.co.uk

DOLPHIN INN
Kingston, Near Kingsbridge,
Devon TQ7 4QE
Tel: 01548 810314
www.dolphin-inn.co.uk

MALTSTERS ARMS
Bow Creek, Tuckenhay,
Near Totnes, Devon TQ9 7EQ
Tel: 01803 732350
www.tuckenhay.com

THE CRICKETERS
Clavering, Near Saffron Walden,
Essex CB11 4QT
Tel: 01799 550442
www.thecricketers.co.uk

KING'S HEAD INN
Birdwood, Near Huntley,
Gloucestershire GL19 3EF
Tel: 01452 750348
www.kingsheadbirdwood.co.uk

RHYDSPENCE INN

Whitney-on-Wye, Near Hay-on-Wye,
Herefordshire HR3 6EU
Tel: 01497 831262
www.rhydspence-inn.co.uk

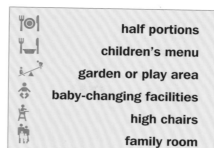

half portions
children's menu
garden or play area
baby-changing facilities
high chairs
family room

SARACENS HEAD INN

Symonds Yat East, Ross-on-Wye,
Herefordshire HR9 6JL
Tel: 01600 890435
www.saracensheadinn.co.uk

CHEQUERS INN

The Street, Smarden,
Near Ashford, Kent TN27 8QA
Tel: 01233 770217
www.thechequerssmarden.com

WHITE HORSE INN

The Street, Boughton,
Kent ME13 9AX
Tel: 01227 751343
www.whitehorsecanterbury.co.uk

WHIPPER-IN HOTEL

Market Place, Oakham,
Leicestershire & Rutland LE15 6DT
Tel: 01572 756971
www.brook-hotels.co.uk

COOK AND BARKER

Newtown-on-the-Moor, Morpeth,
Northumberland NE65 9JY
Tel: 01665 575234
www.cookandbarkerinn.co.uk

TOLLGATE INN

Church Street, Kingham,
Oxfordshire OX7 6YA
Tel: 01608 658389
www.thetollgate.com

THE FLOWER POT

**Ferry Lane, Henley-on-Thames,
Oxfordshire RG9 3DG
Tel: 01491 574721**

MYTTON AND MERMAID

**Atcham, Shrewsbury,
Shropshire SY5 6QG
Tel: 01743 761220
www.myttonandmermaid.co.uk**

THE LAMB INN

**High Street, Hindon
Wiltshire SP3 6DP
Tel: 01747 820573
www.lambathindon.co.uk**

FAIRFAX ARMS

**Gilling East, York,
North Yorkshire YO62 4JH
Tel: 01439 788212
www.fairfaxarms.co.uk**

CARISBROOKE

**Drumduan Road, Forres,
Aberdeen, Banff & Moray IV36 1BS
Tel: 01309 672585
www.carisbrooke-hotel.co.uk**

ABERDOUR HOTEL

**38 High Street, Aberdour,
Fife KY3 0SW
Tel: 01383 860325
www.aberdourhotel.co.uk**

YANN'S AT GLENEARN HOUSE

**Perth Road, Crieff,
Perth & Kinross PH7 3EQ
Tel: 01764 650111
www.yannsatglenearnhouse.com**

CASTLE VIEW HOTEL

**16 Bridge Street, Chepstow,
Monmouthshire NP16 5EZ
Tel: 01291 620349
www.hotelchepstow.co.uk**

MUSEUM OF LONDON DOCKLANDS
No1 Warehouse, West India Quay, London E14 4AL
Tel: 0870 444 3855 • e-mail: info@museumoflondon.org.uk
www.museumoflondon.org.uk

READERS'
OFFER
2009

This voucher entitles the bearer to TWO full price adult tickets for the price of ONE on presentation at the Museum of London Docklands admission desk. A max. of one person goes free per voucher. Offer valid until 31 Dec. 2009. Only one voucher per transaction. Non-transferable and non-exchangeable. No cash alternative. Subject to availability. Tickets allow unlimited entry for one year. Children enter free as standard all year round.

LEIGHTON BUZZARD RAILWAY
Page's Park Station, Billington Road,
Leighton Buzzard, Bedfordshire LU7 4TN
Tel: 01525 373888
e-mail: station@lbngrs.org.uk
www.buzzrail.co.uk

READERS'
OFFER
2009

One FREE adult/child with full-fare adult ticket
Valid 15/3/2009 - 8/11/2009

NOT TO BE USED IN CONJUNCTION WITH ANY OTHER OFFER

BUCKINGHAMSHIRE RAILWAY CENTRE
Quainton Road Station, Quainton,
Aylesbury HP22 4BY
Tel & Fax: 01296 655720
e-mail: bucksrailcentre@btconnect.com
www.bucksrailcentre.org

READERS'
OFFER
2009

One child FREE with each full-paying adult
Not valid for Special Events

NOT TO BE USED IN CONJUNCTION WITH ANY OTHER OFFER

BEKONSCOT MODEL VILLAGE & RAILWAY
Warwick Road, Beaconsfield,
Buckinghamshire HP9 2PL
Tel: 01494 672919
e-mail: info@bekonscot.co.uk
www.bekonscot.com

READERS'
OFFER
2009

One child FREE when accompanied by full-paying adult
Valid February to October 2009

NOT TO BE USED IN CONJUNCTION WITH ANY OTHER OFFER

From Roman settlement to Dockland's regeneration, unlock the history of London's river, port and people in this historic West India Quay warehouse. Discover a wealth of objects, from whalebones to WWII gas masks, in state-of-the-art galleries, including Mudlarks, an interactive area for children; Sailortown, an atmospheric re-creation of 19thC riverside Wapping; and London, Sugar & Slavery, which reveals the city's involvement in the transatlantic slave trade.

Open: daily 10am-6pm. Closed 24-26 December.

Directions: 2 minutes' walk from West India Quay. Nearest Tube Canary Wharf.

A 70-minute journey into the lost world of the English narrow gauge light railway. Features historic steam locomotives from many countries.

PETS MUST BE KEPT UNDER CONTROL AND NOT ALLOWED ON TRACKS

Open: Sundays and Bank Holiday weekends 22 March to 25 October. Additional days in summer.

Directions: on south side of Leighton Buzzard. Follow brown signs from town centre or A505/A4146 bypass.

A working steam railway centre. Steam train rides, miniature railway rides, large collection of historic preserved steam locomotives, carriages and wagons.

Open: daily April to October 10.30am to 4.30pm. Variable programme - check website or call.

Directions: off A41 Aylesbury to Bicester Road, 6 miles north west of Aylesbury.

Be a giant in a magical miniature world of make-believe depicting rural England in the 1930s. "A little piece of history that is forever England."

Open: 10am-5pm daily mid February to end October.

Directions: Junction 16 M25, Junction 2 M40.

Birds of Prey Centre offering audience participation in flying displays which are held 3 times daily. Tours, picnic area, gift shop, tearoom, craft shop.

Open: 10am-5pm all year except Christmas and New Year.

Directions: follow brown tourist signs from B1040.

Home to a unique ancient wooden monument, a km long causeway and platform, perfectly preserved in the wetland. Originally built from 60,000 upright timbers and 250,000 horizontal timbers. Also visit roundhouses, fields and museum.

Open: March to October 10am to 5pm Tuesday to Sunday. Last entry 4pm.

Directions: by bicycle or on foot from the Green Wheel. By car from J5 of A1139, Peterborough ring road, then follow the brown signs.

As seen on TV, this multi award-winning attraction has a great deal to offer visitors. It houses the largest collection of engines in Europe, local history area, craft centre (bodging and smithy work), with changing exhibitions throughout the season.

Open: Easter Sunday until end October, Friday to Sunday and Bank Holidays, 10am to 5pm.

Directions: approx 7 miles from J1 M60 and 9 miles J3 M60. Follow brown tourist signs from Poynton traffic lights.

The nation's foremost and largest museum of historic cycling, with over 400 examples of cycles, and 1000s of items of cycling memorabilia.

Open: all year, Sunday to Thursday, 10am to 5pm.

Directions: one mile north of Camelford, B3266/B3314 crossroads.

CHINA CLAY COUNTRY PARK
Wheal Martyn, Carthew, St Austell,
Cornwall PL26 8XG
Tel & Fax: 01726 850362
e-mail: info@chinaclaycountry.co.uk
www.chinaclaycountry.co.uk

READERS' OFFER 2009

TWO for ONE adult entry, saving £7.50.
One voucher per person. Valid until July 2009.

NOT TO BE USED IN CONJUNCTION WITH ANY OTHER OFFER

NATIONAL LOBSTER HATCHERY
South Quay, Padstow,
Cornwall PL28 8BL
Tel: 01841 533877 • Fax: 0870 7060299
e-mail: info@nationallobsterhatchery.co.uk
www.nationallobsterhatchery.co.uk

READERS' OFFER 2009

TWO for the price of ONE
Valid November 2008 to March 2009

NOT TO BE USED IN CONJUNCTION WITH ANY OTHER OFFER

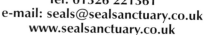

NATIONAL SEAL SANCTUARY
Gweek, Helston,
Cornwall TR12 6UG
Tel: 01326 221361
e-mail: seals@sealsanctuary.co.uk
www.sealsanctuary.co.uk

READERS' OFFER 2009

TWO for ONE - on purchase of another ticket of
equal or greater value. Valid until December 2009.

NOT TO BE USED IN CONJUNCTION WITH ANY OTHER OFFER

PORFELL WILDLIFE PARK & SANCTUARY
Trecangate, Near Llanreath,
Liskeard,
Cornwall PL14 4RE
Tel: 01503 220211
www.porfellanimalland.co.uk

READERS' OFFER 2009

One child FREE with one paying adult per voucher
Valid 1st April-31st October 2009.

NOT TO BE USED IN CONJUNCTION WITH ANY OTHER OFFER

The Country Park covers 26 acres and includes woodland and historic trails, picnic sites, children's adventure trail and award-winning cycle trail. Remains of a Victorian clay works complete with the largest working water wheel in Cornwall. Shop, cafe, exhibitions, museum.

Open: 10am-6pm daily (closed Christmas Day)

Directions: two miles north of St Austell on the B3274. Follow brown tourist signs. 5 minutes from Eden Project.

A unique conservation programme - see our fisheries at work and find out everything there is to know about the European lobster.

Open: from 10am seven days a week.

Directions: right on the water's edge, in the South Quay car park, right opposite Rick Stein's fish & chip shop.

Britain's leading grey seal rescue centre

Open: daily (except Christmas Day) from 10am

Directions: from A30 follow signs to Helston, then brown tourist signs to Seal Sanctuary.

Porfell is home to wild and exotic animals from around the world. Idyllically situated amongst the rolling hills of south east Cornwall. It has a beautiful woodland with raised boardwalks over marsh areas, and a children's farm.

Open: 10am-6pm daily from April 1st to October 31st.

Directions: A38 Liskeard, A390 for St Austell. Turn off at East Taphouse on to B3359, follow brown tourist signs.

TAMAR VALLEY DONKEY PARK
St Ann's Chapel, Gunnislake,
Cornwall PL18 9HW
Tel: 01822 834072
e-mail: info@donkeypark.com
www.donkeypark.com

50p OFF per person, up to 6 persons
Valid from Easter until end October 2009

CARS OF THE STARS MOTOR MUSEUM
Standish Street, Keswick,
Cumbria CA12 5HH
Tel: 017687 73757
e-mail: cotsmm@aol.com
www.carsofthestars.com

One child free with two paying adults
Valid during 2009

THE BEACON
West Strand, Whitehaven,
Cumbria CA28 7LY
Tel: 01946 592302 • Fax: 01946 598150
e-mail: thebeacon@copelandbc.gov.uk
www.thebeacon-whitehaven.co.uk

One FREE adult/concesssion when accompanied by one full paying
adult/concession. Under 16s free. Valid from Oct 08 to end 09.
Not valid for special events. Day tickets only.

CRICH TRAMWAY VILLAGE
Crich, Matlock
Derbyshire DE4 5DP
Tel: 01773 854321 • Fax: 01773 854320
e-mail: enquiry@tramway.co.uk
www.tramway.co.uk

One child FREE with every full-paying adult
Valid during 2009

194

Cornwall's only Donkey Sanctuary set in 14 acres overlooking the beautiful Tamar Valley. Donkey rides, goat hill, children's playgrounds, cafe and picnic area. New all-weather play barn.

Open: Easter to end Oct: daily 10am to 5pm. Nov to March: weekends and all school holidays 10.30am to 4.30pm

Directions: just off A390 between Callington and Gunnislake at St Ann's Chapel.

A collection of cars from film and TV, including Chitty Chitty Bang Bang, James Bond's Aston Martin, Del Boy's van, Fab1 and many more.

PETS MUST BE KEPT ON LEAD

Open: daily 10am-5pm. Open February half term, 1st April to end November, also weekends in December.

Directions: in centre of Keswick close to car park.

The Beacon is the Copeland area's interactive museum, tracing the area's rich history, from as far back as prehistoric times to the modern day. Enjoy panoramic views of the Georgian town and harbour from the 4th floor viewing gallery. Art gallery, gift shop, restaurant. Fully accessible.

Open: open all year (excl. 24-26 Dec) Tuesday to Sunday, plus Monday Bank Holidays.

Directions: enter Whitehaven from north or south on A595. Follow the town centre and brown museum signs; located on harbourside.

A superb family day out in the atmosphere of a bygone era. Explore the recreated period street and fascinating exhibitions. Unlimited tram rides are free with entry. Play areas, woodland walk and sculpture trail, shops, tea rooms, pub, restaurant and lots more.

Open: daily April to October 10 am to 5.30pm.

Directions: eight miles from M1 Junction 28, follow brown and white signs for "Tramway Museum".

POOLE'S CAVERN & BUXTON COUNTRY PARK

Green Lane, Buxton,
Derbyshire Sk17 9DH
Tel: 01298 26978 • Fax: 01298 73563
e-mail: info@poolescavern.co.uk
www.poolescavern.co.uk

READERS' OFFER 2009

20% off standard entry price to Poole's Cavern.
Not valid for special events. Valid during 2009.

NOT TO BE USED IN CONJUNCTION WITH ANY OTHER OFFER

WOODLANDS

Blackawton, Dartmouth,
Devon TQ9 7DQ
Tel: 01803 712598 • Fax: 01803 712680
e-mail: fun@woodlandspark.com
www.woodlandspark.com

READERS' OFFER 2009

12% discount off individual entry price for up to 4
persons. No photocopies. Valid 4/4/09 – 1/11/09

NOT TO BE USED IN CONJUNCTION WITH ANY OTHER OFFER

DEVONSHIRE COLLECTION OF PERIOD COSTUME

Totnes Costume Museum,
Bogan House, 43 High Street,
Totnes,
Devon TQ9 5NP

READERS' OFFER 2009

FREE child with a paying adult with voucher
Valid from Spring Bank Holiday to end of Sept 2009

NOT TO BE USED IN CONJUNCTION WITH ANY OTHER OFFER

TWEDDLE CHILDREN'S ANIMAL FARM

Fillpoke Lane, Blackhall Colliery,
Co. Durham TS27 4BT
Tel: 0191 586 3311
e-mail: info@tweddle-farm.co.uk
www.tweddle-farm.co.uk

READERS' OFFER 2009

FREE bag of animal food to every paying customer.
Valid until end 2009

NOT TO BE USED IN CONJUNCTION WITH ANY OTHER OFFER

196

A spectacular natural cavern set in beautiful woodlands. Explore the crystal-lined chambers with expert guides, deep into the Peak District underground world. Climb to Solomon's Temple viewpoint at the summit of Grin Low.

Open: daily March to November 9.30am to 5pm; winter weekends.

Directions: one mile from Buxton town centre, off A515.

All weather fun - guaranteed! Unique combination of indoor/outdoor attractions. 3 Watercoasters, Toboggan Run, Arctic Gliders, boats, 15 Playzones for all ages. Biggest indoor venture zone in UK with 5 floors of play and rides. Big Fun Farm with U-drive Tractor ride, new Sea Dragon Swing Ship. Falconry Centre.

Open: mid-March to November open daily at 9.30am. Winter: open weekends and local school holidays.

Directions: 5 miles from Dartmouth on A3122. Follow brown tourist signs from A38.

Themed exhibition, changed annually, based in a Tudor house. Collection contains items of dress for women, men and children from 17th century to 1990s, from high fashion to everyday wear.

Open: Open from Spring Bank Holiday to end September. 11am to 5pm Tuesday to Friday.

Directions: centre of town, opposite Market Square. Mini bus up High Street stops outside.

Children's farm and petting centre with lots of farm animals and exotic animals too, including camels, otters, monkeys, meerkats and lots more. Lots of hands-on, with bottle feeding, reptile handling and bunny cuddling happening daily.

Open: March to Oct: 10am-5pm daily; Nov to Feb 10am to 4pm daily. Closed Christmas, Boxing Day and New Year's Day.

Directions: A181 from A19, head towards coast; signposted from there.

**READERS'
OFFER
2009**

BARLEYLANDS FARM & CRAFT VILLAGE
Barleylands Road, Billericay,
Essex CM11 2UD
Tel: 01268 290229 • Fax: 01268 290222
e-mail: info@barleylands.co.uk
www.barleylands.co.uk

BARLEYLANDS

> *FREE entry for one child with each full paying adult*
> *Valid during 2009*

NOT TO BE USED IN CONJUNCTION WITH ANY OTHER OFFER

**READERS'
OFFER
2009**

AVON VALLEY RAILWAY
Bitton Station, Bath Road, Bitton,
Bristol BS30 6HD
Tel: 0117 932 5538
e-mail: info@avonvalleyrailway.org
www.avonvalleyrailway.org

> *One FREE child with every fare-paying adult*
> *Valid May - Oct 2009 (not 'Day Out with Thomas' events)*

NOT TO BE USED IN CONJUNCTION WITH ANY OTHER OFFER

**READERS'
OFFER
2009**

CIDER MUSEUM & KING OFFA DISTILLERY
21 Ryelands Street, Hereford,
Herefordshire HR4 0LW
Tel: 01432 354207
e-mail: enquiries@cidermuseum.co.uk
www.cidermuseum.co.uk

> *TWO for the price of ONE admission*
> *Valid to end December 2009*

NOT TO BE USED IN CONJUNCTION WITH ANY OTHER OFFER

FHG
·K·U·P·E·R·A·R·D·
**READERS'
OFFER
2009**

MUSEUM OF KENT LIFE
Lock Lane, Sandling, Maidstone,
Kent ME14 3AU
Tel: 01622 763936 • Fax: 01622 662024
e-mail: enquiries@museum-kentlife.co.uk
www.museum-kentlife.co.uk

MUSEUM OF
KENT LIFE

> *One child FREE with one full-paying adult*
> *Valid during 2009*

NOT TO BE USED IN CONJUNCTION WITH ANY OTHER OFFER

Set in over 700 acres of unspoilt Essex countryside, this former working farm is one of the county's most popular tourist attractions. The spectacular craft village and educational farm provide the perfect setting for a great day out.

Open: 7 days a week from 10am-5pm all year except 25/26 December and 1st January

Directions: follow brown tourist signs from A127 and A12.

The Avon Valley Railway offers a whole new experience for some, and a nostalgic memory for others.

PETS MUST BE KEPT ON LEADS AND OFF TRAIN SEATS

Open: Steam trains operate every Sunday, Easter to October, plus Bank Holidays and Christmas.

Directions: on the A431 midway between Bristol and Bath at Bitton.

Learn how traditional cider and perry was made, how the fruit was harvested, milled, pressed and bottled. Walk through original champagne cider cellars, and view 18th century lead crystal cider glasses.

Open: April to October: 10am-5pm Tues-Sat. November to March 11am-3pm Tues-Sat.

Directions: off A438 Hereford to Brecon road, near Sainsbury's supermarket.

Kent's award-winning open air museum is home to a collection of historic buildings which house interactive exhibitions on life over the last 150 years.

Open: seven days a week, February to start November, 10am to 5pm.

Directions: Junction 6 off M20, follow signs to Aylesford.

CHISLEHURST CAVES
Old Hill, Chislehurst,
Kent BR7 5NL
Tel: 020 8467 3264 • Fax: 020 8295 0407
e-mail: info@chislehurstcaves.co.uk
www.chislehurstcaves.co.uk

READERS' OFFER 2009

FREE child entry with full paying adult.
Valid until end 2009 (not Bank Holiday weekends)

NOT TO BE USED IN CONJUNCTION WITH ANY OTHER OFFER

SKEGNESS NATURELAND SEAL SANCTUARY
North Parade, Skegness,
Lincolnshire PE25 1DB
Tel: 01754 764345
e-mail: info@skegnessnatureland.co.uk
www.skegnessnatureland.co.uk

Natureland Seal Sanctuary

READERS' OFFER 2009

Free entry for one child when accompanied by full-paying adult. Valid during 2009.

NOT TO BE USED IN CONJUNCTION WITH ANY OTHER OFFER

BRESSINGHAM STEAM & GARDENS
Low Road, Bressingham, Diss,
Norfolk IP22 2AB
Tel: 01379 686900 • Fax: 01379 686907
e-mail: info@bressingham.co.uk
www.bressingham.co.uk

READERS' OFFER 2009

One child FREE with two paying adults
Valid Easter to October 2009 (ref 8175)

NOT TO BE USED IN CONJUNCTION WITH ANY OTHER OFFER

NEWARK AIR MUSEUM
The Airfield, Winthorpe, Newark,
Nottinghamshire NG24 2NY
Tel: 01636 707170
e-mail: newarkair@onetel.com
www.newarkairmuseum.org

READERS' OFFER 2009

Party rate discount for every voucher (50p per person off normal admission). Valid during 2009.

NOT TO BE USED IN CONJUNCTION WITH ANY OTHER OFFER

Miles of mystery and history beneath your feet! Grab a lantern and get ready for an amazing underground adventure. Your whole family can travel back in time as you explore this labyrinth of dark mysterious passageways. See the caves, church, Druid altar and more.

Open: Wed to Sun from 10am; last tour 4pm. Open daily during local school and Bank holidays (except Christmas). Entrance by guided tour only.

Directions: A222 between A20 and A21; at Chislehurst Station turn into Station Approach; turn right at end, then right again into Caveside Close.

FHG GUIDES, ABBEY MILL BUSINESS CENTRE, PAISLEY PA1 1TJ • www.holidayguides.com

---

Well known for rescuing and rehabilitating orphaned and injured seal pups found washed ashore on Lincolnshire beaches. Also: penguins, aquarium, pets' corner, reptiles, Floral Palace (tropical birds and butterflies etc).

Open: daily from 10am. Closed Christmas/Boxing/New Year's Days.

Directions: at the north end of Skegness seafront.

FHG GUIDES, ABBEY MILL BUSINESS CENTRE, PAISLEY PA1 1TJ • www.holidayguides.com

---

Explore one of Europe's leading steam collections, take a ride over 5 miles of narrow gauge steam railway, wander through beautiful gardens, or visit the only official 'Dads' Army' exhibition. Two restaurants and garden centre.

Open: Easter to October 10.30am - 5pm

Directions: 2½ miles west of Diss and 14 miles east of Thetford on the A1066; follow brown tourist signs.

FHG GUIDES, ABBEY MILL BUSINESS CENTRE, PAISLEY PA1 1TJ • www.holidayguides.com

---

A collection of 70 aircraft and cockpit sections from across the history of aviation. Extensive aero engine and artefact displays.

Open: daily from 10am (closed Christmas period and New Year's Day).

Directions: follow brown and white signs from A1, A46, A17 and A1133.

FHG GUIDES, ABBEY MILL BUSINESS CENTRE, PAISLEY PA1 1TJ • www.holidayguides.com

Enter and explore these ancient caves and see how the people of Nottingham have used them for over 750 years.

Open: daily 10.30-5pm (tours every half hour).

Directions: in Nottingham city centre on the upper level of Broadmarsh Shopping Centre.

Let us welcome you to Nottingham's notorious county gaol, and once behind bars, our resident ghosts won't want you to leave!

Open: peak season - daily 10am-5pm; off peak Tues - Sun 10am-4pm. Tours every half hour.

Directions: in the heart of the historic Lace Market district, just 10 minutes' walk from train station.

Family-run farm park set in beautiful countryside next to river. 20-acre site with animal handling, large indoor soft play area, go-karts, trampolines, pedal tractors, swings, slides, zipline and assault course. New Jumicar children's driving activity (small extra charge)

Open: daily 10am to 5.30pm April to end September. Closed Mondays except Bank Holidays and during Nottinghamshire school holidays. Please check for winter opening hours.

Directions: off A612 Nottingham to Southwell road.

Travel back in time with Robin Hood and his merry men on an adventure-packed theme tour, exploring the intriguing and mysterious story of their legendary tales of Medieval England. Enjoy film shows, live performances, adventure rides and even try archery! Are you brave enough to join Robin on his quest for good against evil?

Open: 10am-5pm, last admission 4pm.

Directions: follow the brown and white tourist information signs whilst heading towards the city centre.

203

FLEET AIR ARM MUSEUM

RNAS Yeovilton, Ilchester,
Somerset BA22 8HT
Tel: 01935 840565
e-mail: enquiries@fleetairarm.com
www.fleetairarm.com

One child FREE with full paying adult
Valid during 2009 except Bank Holidays

THE HELICOPTER MUSEUM

The Heliport, Locking Moor Road,
Weston-Super-Mare BS24 8PP
Tel: 01934 635227• Fax: 01934 645230
e-mail: helimuseum@btconnect.com
www.helicoptermuseum.co.uk

One child FREE with two full-paying adults
Valid from April to October 2009

EXMOOR FALCONRY & ANIMAL FARM

Allerford, Near Porlock, Minehead,
Somerset TA24 8HJ
Tel: 01643 862816
e-mail: exmoor.falcon@virgin.net
www.exmoorfalconry.co.uk

10% off entry to Falconry Centre
Valid during 2009

EASTON FARM PARK

Pound Corner, Easton, Woodhouse,
Suffolk IP13 0EQ
Tel: 01728 746475
e-mail: info@eastonfarmpark.co.uk
www.eastonfarmpark.co.uk

Easton
Farm Park

One FREE child entry with a full paying adult
Only one voucher per group. Valid during 2009.

Europe's largest naval aviation collection with over 40 aircraft on display , including Concorde 002 and Ark Royal Aircraft Carrier Experience. Situated on an operational naval air station.

Open: open daily April to October 10am-5.30pm; November to March 10am-4.30pm (closed Mon and Tues).

Directions: just off A303/A37 on B3151 at Ilchester. Yeovil rail station 10 miles.

FHG GUIDES, ABBEY MILL BUSINESS CENTRE, PAISLEY PA1 1TJ • www.holidayguides.com

---

The world's largest helicopter collection - over 70 exhibits, includes two royal helicopters, Russian Gunship and Vietnam veterans plus many award-winning exhibits. Cafe, shop. Flights.

PETS MUST BE KEPT UNDER CONTROL

Open: Wednesday to Sunday 10am to 5.30pm. Daily during school Easter and Summer holidays and Bank Holiday Mondays. November to March: 10am to 4.30pm

Directions: Junction 21 off M5 then follow the propellor signs.

FHG GUIDES, ABBEY MILL BUSINESS CENTRE, PAISLEY PA1 1TJ • www.holidayguides.com

---

Falconry centre with animals - flying displays, animal handling, feeding and bottle feeding - in 15th century NT farmyard setting on Exmoor. Also falconry and outdoor activities, hawk walks and riding.

Open: 10.30am to 5pm daily

Directions: A39 west of Minehead, turn right at Allerford, half a mile along lane on left.

FHG GUIDES, ABBEY MILL BUSINESS CENTRE, PAISLEY PA1 1TJ • www.holidayguides.com

---

Family day out down on the farm, with activities for children every half hour (included in entry price). Indoor and outdoor play areas. Riverside cafe, gift shop. For more details visit the website.

Open: 10.30am-6pm daily March to September.

Directions: signposted from A12 in the direction of Framlingham.

FHG GUIDES, ABBEY MILL BUSINESS CENTRE, PAISLEY PA1 1TJ • www.holidayguides.com

Stories of racing, ride the horse simulator, or take a 'behind the scenes' tour of the training grounds and yards.

Open: Easter to end October, 7 days a week 11am to 5pm. Last admission 4pm.

Directions: on the High Street in the centre of Newmarket.

3 attractions in 1.
Tropical butterflies, exotic animals of many types in our Noah's Ark Rescue Centre. Theme gardens with a free competition for kids. Rejectamenta - the nostalgia museum.

Open: 10am - 6pm daily late March to end October.

Directions: signposted from A27/A286 junction at Chichester.

Hatton Farm Village offers a wonderful mix of farmyard animals, adventure play, shows, demonstrations, and events, all set in the stunning Warwickshire countryside.

Open: daily 10am-5pm (4pm during winter). Closed Christmas Day and Boxing Day.

Directions: 5 minutes from M40 (J15), A46 towards Coventry, then just off A4177 (follow brown tourist signs).

Birds of prey centre with over 60 birds including owls, hawks, falcons, kites, vultures and eagles. 3 flying displays daily.
When possible public welcome to handle birds after each display. No dogs allowed.

Open: 1st March to 31st October 10.30am to 5.30pm. Flying displays 11.30am, 1.30pm and 3.30pm daily.

Directions: on the A167 between Northallerton and the Ripon turn off. Follow brown tourist signs.

YORKSHIRE DALES FALCONRY & WILDLIFE CONSERVATION CENTRE
Crow's Nest, Giggleswick, Near Settle LA2 8AS
Tel: 01729 822832• Fax: 01729 825160
e-mail: info@falconryandwildlife.com
www.falconryandwildlife.com

YORKSHIRE DALES FALCONRY & WILDLIFE CONSERVATION CENTRE

READERS' OFFER 2009

One child FREE with two full-paying adults
Valid until end 2009

NOT TO BE USED IN CONJUNCTION WITH ANY OTHER OFFER

WORLD OF JAMES HERRIOT
23 Kirkgate, Thirsk,
North Yorkshire YO7 1PL
Tel: 01845 524234
Fax: 01845 525333
www.worldofjamesherriot.org

HERRIOT

READERS' OFFER 2009

Admit TWO for the price of ONE (one voucher per transaction only). Valid until October 2009

NOT TO BE USED IN CONJUNCTION WITH ANY OTHER OFFER

MUSEUM OF RAIL TRAVEL
Ingrow Railway Centre, Near Keighley,
West Yorkshire BD21 5AX
Tel: 01535 680425
e-mail: admin@vintagecarriagestrust.org
www.vintagecarriagestrust.org

READERS' OFFER 2009

"ONE for ONE" free admission
Valid during 2009 except during special events (ring to check)

NOT TO BE USED IN CONJUNCTION WITH ANY OTHER OFFER

EUREKA! THE MUSEUM FOR CHILDREN
Discovery Road, Halifax,
West Yorkshire HX1 2NE
Tel: 01422 330069 • Fax: 01422 398490
e-mail: info@eureka.org.uk
www.eureka.org.uk

EUREKA! the museum for children

READERS' OFFER 2009

One FREE child on purchase of full price adult ticket
Valid from 1/10/08 to 31/12/09. Excludes groups.

NOT TO BE USED IN CONJUNCTION WITH ANY OTHER OFFER

All types of birds of prey exhibited here, from owls and kestrels to eagles and vultures. Special flying displays 12 noon, 1.30pm and 3pm. Winter shows 12noon and 1.30pm. Bird handling courses arranged for either half or full days.

GUIDE DOGS ONLY

Open: 10am to 4.30pm summer 10am to 4pm winter

Directions: on main A65 trunk road outside Settle. Follow brown direction signs.

Visit James Herriot's original house recreated as it was in the 1940s. Television sets used in the series 'All Creatures Great and Small'. There is a children's interactive gallery with life-size model farm animals and three rooms dedicated to the history of veterinary medicine.

Open: daily. Easter-Oct 10am-5pm; Nov-Easter 11am to 4pm

Directions: follow signs off A1 or A19 to Thirsk, then A168, off Thirsk market place

---

A fascinating display of railway carriages and a wide range of railway items telling the story of rail travel over the years.

ALL PETS MUST BE KEPT ON LEADS

Open: daily 11am to 4.30pm

Directions: approximately one mile from Keighley on A629 Halifax road. Follow brown tourist signs

---

As the UK's National Children's Museum, Eureka! is a place where children play to learn and grown-ups learn to play.

Open: daily except 24-26 December, 10am to 5pm

Directions: leave M62 at J24 for Halifax. Take A629 to town centre, following brown tourist signs.

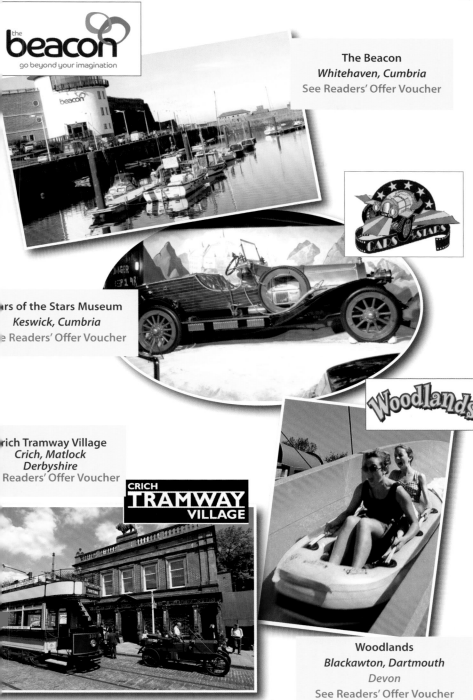

The Beacon
Whitehaven, Cumbria
See Readers' Offer Voucher

...rs of the Stars Museum
Keswick, Cumbria
...e Readers' Offer Voucher

...rich Tramway Village
Crich, Matlock
Derbyshire
...Readers' Offer Voucher

Woodlands
Blackawton, Dartmouth
Devon
See Readers' Offer Voucher

GALLOWAY WILDLIFE CONSERVATION PARK

Galloway Wildlife Conservation Park
Lochfergus, Kirkcudbright,
Dumfries & Galloway
See Readers' Offer Voucher

RHEILFFORDD
LLYN PADARN
LLANBERIS LAKE
RAILWAY

Llanberis Lake Railway
Gilfach Ddu, Llanberis, Gwynedd
See Readers' Offer Voucher

Felinwynt Rainforest Cer
Cardigan, Ceredigion
See Readers' Offer Vouc

Visitor Centre dedicated to the much-loved Scottish writer Lewis Grassic Gibbon. Exhibition, cafe, gift shop. Outdoor children's play area. Disabled access throughout.

Open: daily April to October 10am to 4.30pm. Groups by appointment including evenings.

Directions: on the B967, accessible and signposted from both A90 and A92.

Scotland's seafaring heritage is among the world's richest and you can relive the heyday of Scottish shipping at the Maritime Museum.

Open: 1st April to 31st October - 10am-5pm

Directions: situated on Irvine harbourside and only a 10 minute walk from Irvine train station.

Indoor adventure play area, farm park, toyshop and cafe. A great day out for all the family, with sledge and zip slides, mini-golf, trampolines, bumper boats, pottery painting and so much more.

Open: Monday to Saturday 10am-5.30pm.

Directions: just off the A75/A701 roundabout heading for Moffat and Edinburgh.

The wild animal conservation centre of Southern Scotland. A varied collection of over 150 animals from all over the world can be seen within natural woodland settings. Picnic areas, cafe/gift shop, outdoor play area, woodland walks, close animal encounters.

Open: 10am to dusk 1st February to 30 November.

Directions: follow brown tourist signs from A75; one mile from Kirkcudbright on the B727.

213

CREETOWN GEM ROCK MUSEUM
Chain Road, Creetown, Newton Stewart
Dumfries & Galloway DG8 7HJ
Tel: 01671 820357 • Fax: 01671 820554
e-mail: enquiries@gemrock.net
www.gemrock.net

READERS' OFFER 2009

10% discount on admission.
Valid during 2009.

NOT TO BE USED IN CONJUNCTION WITH ANY OTHER OFFER

MYRETON MOTOR MUSEUM
Aberlady,
East Lothian
EH32 0PZ
Tel: 01875 870288

READERS' OFFER 2009

One child FREE with each paying adult
Valid during 2009

NOT TO BE USED IN CONJUNCTION WITH ANY OTHER OFFER

BO'NESS & KINNEIL RAILWAY
Bo'ness Station, Union Street,
Bo'ness, West Lothian EH51 9AQ
Tel: 01506 822298
e-mail: enquiries.railway@srps.org.uk
www.srps.org.uk

READERS' OFFER 2009

FREE child train fare with one paying adult/concession. Valid 29th
March-26th Oct 2009. Not Thomas events or Santa Steam trains

NOT TO BE USED IN CONJUNCTION WITH ANY OTHER OFFER

BUTTERFLY & INSECT WORLD
Dobbies Garden World, Melville Nursery,
Lasswade, Midlothian EH18 1AZ
Tel: 0131-663 4932 • Fax: 0131-654 2774
e-mail: info@edinburgh-butterfly-world.co.uk
www.edinburgh-butterfly-world.co.uk

READERS' OFFER 2009

£1.50 OFF full adult admission (max. 2 adults per voucher)
Photocopies not accepted. Valid during 2009.

NOT TO BE USED IN CONJUNCTION WITH ANY OTHER OFFER

A fantastic display of gems, crystals, minerals and fossils. An experience you'll treasure forever. Gift shop, tearoom and AV display.

Open: Summer - 9.30am to 5.30pm daily; Winter - 10am to 4pm daily. Closed Christmas to end January.

Directions: follow signs from A75 Dumfries/Stranraer.

On show is a large collection, from 1899, of cars, bicycles, motor cycles and commercials. There is also a large collection of period advertising, posters and enamel signs.

Open: March-November - open daily 11am to 4pm. December-February - weekends 11am to 3pm or by special appointment.

Directions: off A198 near Aberlady. Two miles from A1.

Steam and heritage diesel passenger trains from Bo'ness to Birkhill for guided tours of Birkhill fireclay mines. Explore the history of Scotland's railways in the Scottish Railway Exhibition. Coffee shop and souvenir shop.

Open: weekends Easter to October, daily July and August.

Directions: in the town of Bo'ness. Leave M9 at Junction 3 or 5, then follow brown tourist signs.

See free-flying exotic butterflies in a tropical rainforest paradise. Have close encounters of the crawly kind in the 'Bugs & Beasties' exhibition that includes arrow frogs, tarantulas, amazing leaf-cutter ants and a unique seasonal Scottish Honey Bee display.

Open: daily. 9.30am-5.30pm summer, 10am-5pm winter.

Directions: located just off the Edinburgh City Bypass at the Gilmerton exit or at the Sherrifhall roundabout.

215

The story of Glasgow and the River Clyde brought vividly to life using AV, hands-on and interactive techniques. You can navigate your own ship, safely load your cargo, operate an engine, and go aboard the 130-year-old coaster 'Kyles'. Ideal for kids young and old wanting an exciting day out. New - The Clyde's Navy.

Open: 10am to 5.30pm daily

Directions: Green Car Park near M&S at Braehead Shopping Centre.

FHG GUIDES, ABBEY MILL BUSINESS CENTRE, PAISLEY PA1 1TJ • www.holidayguides.com

Award-winning attraction with unique 'Heather Story' exhibition, gallery, giftshop, large garden centre selling 300 different heathers, antique shop, children's play area and famous Clootie Dumpling restaurant.

Open: all year except Christmas Day and New Year's Day.

Directions: just off A95 between Aviemore and Grantown-on-Spey.

FHG GUIDES, ABBEY MILL BUSINESS CENTRE, PAISLEY PA1 1TJ • www.holidayguides.com

218

A 60-minute ride along the shores of beautiful Padarn Lake behind a quaint historic steam engine. Magnificent views of the mountains from lakeside picnic spots.

DOGS MUST BE KEPT ON LEAD AT ALL TIMES ON TRAIN

Open: most days Easter to October. Free timetable leaflet on request.

Directions: just off A4086 Caernarfon to Capel Curig road at Llanberis; follow 'Country Park' signs.

FHG GUIDES, ABBEY MILL BUSINESS CENTRE, PAISLEY PA1 1TJ • www.holidayguides.com

---

Mini-rainforest full of tropical plants and exotic butterflies. Personal attention of the owner, Mr John Devereux. Gift shop, cafe, video room, exhibition. Suitable for disabled visitors. VisitWales Quality Assured Visitor Attraction.

PETS NOT ALLOWED IN TROPICAL HOUSE ONLY

Open: daily Easter to end October 10.30am to 5pm

Directions: West Wales, 7 miles north of Cardigan off Aberystwyth road. Follow brown tourist signs on A487.

FHG GUIDES, ABBEY MILL BUSINESS CENTRE, PAISLEY PA1 1TJ • www.holidayguides.com

---

Journey through the lanes of cycle history and see bicycles from Boneshakers and Penny Farthings up to modern Raleigh cycles. Over 250 machines on display

PETS MUST BE KEPT ON LEADS

Open: 1st March to 1st November daily 10am onwards.

Directions: brown signs to car park. Town centre attraction.

FHG GUIDES, ABBEY MILL BUSINESS CENTRE, PAISLEY PA1 1TJ • www.holidayguides.com

---

Make a pit stop whatever the weather! Join an ex-miner on a tour of discovery, ride the cage to pit bottom and take a thrilling ride back to the surface. Multi-media presentations, period village street, children's adventure play area, restaurant and gift shop. Disabled access with assistance.

Open: Open daily 10am to 6pm (last tour 4pm). Closed Mondays Oct - Easter, also Dec 25th to early Jan.

Directions: Exit Junction 32 M4, signposted from A470 Pontypridd. Trehafod is located between Pontypridd and Porth.

FHG GUIDES, ABBEY MILL BUSINESS CENTRE, PAISLEY PA1 1TJ • www.holidayguides.com

Index of Towns and Counties

Ratings & Awards

For the first time ever the AA, VisitBritain, VisitScotland, and the Wales Tourist Board will use a single method of assessing and rating serviced accommodation. Irrespective of which organisation inspects an establishment the rating awarded will be the same, using a common set of standards, giving a clear guide of what to expect. The RAC is no longer operating an Hotel inspection and accreditation business.

Accommodation Standards: Star Grading Scheme

Using a scale of 1-5 stars the objective quality ratings give a clear indication of accommodation standard, cleanliness, ambience, hospitality, service and food, This shows the full range of standards suitable for every budget and preference, and allows visitors to distinguish between the quality of accommodation and facilities on offer in different establishments. All types of board and self-catering accommodation are covered, including hotels, B&Bs, holiday parks, campus accommodation, hostels, caravans and camping, and boats.

VisitBritain and the regional tourist boards, enjoyEngland.com, VisitScotland and VisitWales, and the AA have full details of the grading system on their websites

The more stars, the higher level of quality

★★★★★
exceptional quality, with a degree of luxury

★★★★
excellent standard throughout

★★★
very good level of quality and comfort

★★
good quality, well presented and well run

★
acceptable quality; simple, practical, no frills

National Accessible Scheme

If you have particular mobility, visual or hearing needs, look out for the National Accessible Scheme. You can be confident of finding accommodation or attractions that meet your needs by looking for the following symbols.

 Typically suitable for a person with sufficient mobility to climb a flight of steps but would benefit from fixtures and fittings to aid balance

 Typically suitable for a person with restricted walking ability and for those that may need to use a wheelchair some of the time and can negotiate a maximum of three steps

 Typically suitable for a person who depends on the use of a wheelchair and transfers unaided to and from the wheelchair in a seated position. This person may be an independent traveller

 Typically suitable for a person who depends on the use of a wheelchair in a seated position. This person also requires personal or mechanical assistance (eg carer, hoist).

Looking for Holiday Accommodation?

for details of hundreds of properties throughout the UK, visit our website

www.holidayguides.com

FHG Guides Ltd have a large range of attractive
holiday accommodation guides for all kinds of holiday opportunities throughout Britain.
They also make useful gifts at any time of year.
Our guides are available in most bookshops and larger newsagents but we will be happy
to post you a copy direct if you have any difficulty. POST FREE for addresses in the UK.
We will also post abroad but have to charge separately for post or freight.

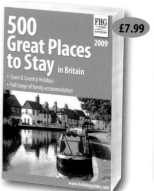

£7.99

£8.99

£9.99

500
Great Places to Stay
in Britain
- Coast & Country Holidays
- Full range of family accommodation

Bed &
Breakfast Stops
in Britain
- For holidaymakers and business travellers
- Overnight stops and Short Breaks

The Golf Guide
Where to play, Where to stay.
- Over 2800 golf courses in Britain with convenient accommodation.
- Holiday Golf in France, Portugal, Spain, USA and Thailand.

£9.99

£6.99

£7.99

The Original
Pets Welcome!
- The bestselling guide to holidays for pets and their owners

Country
Hotels
of Britain
- Hotels with Conference, Leisure and Wedding Facilities

Caravan
& Camping Holidays
in Britain
- Campsites and Caravan parks
- Facilities fully listed

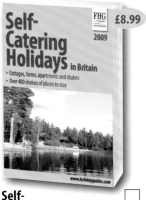

Family Breaks
in Britain
• Accommodation, attractions and resorts
• Suitable for those with children and babies

Self-Catering Holidays
in Britain
• Cottages, farms, apartments and chalets
• Over 400 places to stay

Weekend & Short Breaks
in Britain
• Accommodation for holidays and weekends away

Tick your choice above and send your order and payment to

FHG Guides Ltd. Abbey Mill Business Centre
Seedhill, Paisley, Scotland PA1 1TJ
TEL: 0141- 887 0428 • FAX: 0141- 889 7204
e-mail: admin@fhguides.co.uk

Deduct 10% for 2/3 titles or copies; 20% for 4 or more.

Send to: NAME ....

            ADDRESS ....

            ....

            ....

            POST CODE ....

I enclose Cheque/Postal Order for £ ....

            SIGNATURE ....DATE ....

Please complete the following to help us improve the service we provide.

How did you find out about our guides?:

Press   Magazines   TV/Radio   Family/Friend   Other